DECORATIVE PLASTERCRAFT

a complete guide to making plaster whiteware, casting, carving, sculpturing, painting, and antiquing

B. Kay Fraser

CROWN PUBLISHERS, INC., NEW YORK

OTHER BOOKS BY THE AUTHOR
Creative Bottle Cutting
Decorative Tole Painting

Design by Nedda Balter

Contents

Plastercraft is easy but beautiful. Select a design made of plaster "whiteware" and paint it to suit your individual tastes. Courtesy Off the Wall of Eugene, Ore.

Plastercraft...
Fun for Everyone

What is plastercraft? It's a creative hobby that enables everyone to make beautiful plaques and statues with a minimum of effort and expense.

Plastercraft requires no special talent or previous artistic experience. Yet within a few hours, you can create a plaque of flowers, fruit, guns, children, mushrooms, zodiacs. You can create a piece of statuary such as an animal or bird, a bust of a famous person, candleholders, bookends, and much, much more.

You simply make it yourself or purchase the plaque or statue in "whiteware" form from a hobby store or craft section of a department store. (Whiteware is uncolored, three-dimensional, and usually made of plaster poured in a mold.) Then, in the privacy of your home, you can paint and decorate this form in favorite colors. You can use spray paint, acrylic craft paint, artists' oils—even shoe polish!

The results are breathtaking. A painted piece of plaster whiteware can look as if you've taken days and days to complete it. And you'll feel like an accomplished artist.

Although plastercraft is an extremely easy hobby, it can still challenge the imagination of experienced craftsmen. The variety of ways to decorate plaster is endless. For example, you can paint figurines to look like fine china. Statuary can be painted to duplicate aged marble or hand-carved wood. Plaques can be painted to imitate bronze, copper, silver, and gold.

Plastercraft may even be combined with other crafts for intriguing effects. The whiteware may be tole painted, for instance. Flat plaques lend themselves well to découpage work. Many designs are enhanced by glass staining. Gold leafing is another possibility.

And that is the purpose of this book: to explore step by step the many avenues a plastercraft artist may take. With instructions given here, you can easily create professional-looking plaques and statues in your leisure time at home.

But first let's state a few facts about this craft. Its main ingredient is plaster, which is made from gypsum rock. When mined, this rock is hard;

but a heating process rids the rock of water and leaves a soft material that is crushed into a fine white powder. This powder is what we call plaster. When mixed with water, plaster will set or crystallize once more into a hard, white solid similar to the original rock.

This is why plastercraft is so versatile. You can cast or mold the plaster-water mixture into any shape or size imaginable. It can reproduce any mold with perfect detail.

But plastercraft is nothing new. Although its origins are lost in the mists of antiquity, we do know that the use of gypsum as a plaster base for decoration goes back at least five thousand years. Plastered walls and ornamental ceilings have been found in the pyramids of Egypt. There is evidence that the ancient Hebrews, Greeks, and Romans also used plaster for decorative purposes.

Plaster was not produced commercially, however, until about 1750. Gypsum is abundant throughout the world, but the first commercial enterprise began in the suburbs of Paris, France, and that is why it is often called "plaster of Paris."

Plaster available to craftsmen today is much more durable than plaster of Paris, however, because manufacturers have added hardeners and other chemicals. In fact, modern manufacturers are largely responsible for the current rebirth in popularity of plastercraft.

Sophisticated molds are now available so that you can make or buy plaster whiteware in a limitless variety of designs. And the craft industry is now manufacturing an amazing range of paints, sprays, and finishes to decorate plaster. One manufacturer even offers favorite scents to give plaster a long-lasting aroma.

Thus, advanced technology enables us to express our creativity and originality through plastercraft. Unlike olden days, when only artisans worked with plaster, today people of all ages and walks of life can enjoy the craft. Plastercraft now appeals to homemakers, football coaches, professional artists, children, retired persons—anyone who yearns to create an object of beauty.

So welcome to a craft that intrigued ancient artists and fascinates modern craftsmen today—plastercraft.

2

Start with Plaster

The first step in plastercraft is to obtain plaster whiteware, also called "castings," to paint and decorate. Whiteware may be purchased from hobby stores or from the hobby departments of variety stores. Many stores sell plaster products only. Plastercraft outlets can be found in the yellow pages of the telephone book under Plaster Products or Ceramics. (Plastercraft is sometimes referred to as "cold ceramics." However, true ceramics are made of clay and fired in a kiln.)

The selection of plaster whiteware is amazing. You can choose three-dimensional wall plaques of flowers, rifles, faces, mushrooms, owls, zodiacs, animals, ships, clocks, etc. You can choose realistically shaped statuary (forms that stand rather than hang) such as cigar-store Indians, busts of famous persons, fruit compotes, religious figurines, lamp bases, large animals, and even famous sculptures like Michelangelo's "Pietà."

Best yet, plaster whiteware is not expensive. The cost varies from about thirty cents to thirty dollars depending upon the size of your selection. But painting it with imagination can transform whiteware into a costly-looking treasure.

If you wish to paint a variety of plaster designs, it will be easiest to purchase ready-made whiteware from the store. Then skip ahead to the next chapter for instructions on decorating designs. However, it is also fun and easy to make your own plaster whiteware from molds. And this chapter tells you how.

MAKING PLASTER WHITEWARE

Materials needed to make plaster whiteware, or castings, are:

plaster	stirring utensil
water	mold
mixing bucket	clean-up bucket

Plaster can be bought at hobby stores and some hardware stores and lumberyards. It may be called casting plaster, art plaster, plaster of Paris, or may be known under a variety of brand names, such as Hydrocal. More expensive plaster or gypsum cement tends to be harder, stronger, and heavier. A ten-pound bag of plaster should be ample to start with, and unused plaster should be stored in a clean, dry place.

Water should be cool and fit to drink. That is, it should be free from sediment and dissolved chemicals that might affect the setting time of the plaster.

Mixing and clean-up buckets should be disposable or plastic. Disposable containers could be large milkshake cups or gallon milk cartons. Although glass or steel bowls or pitchers may be used, plastic is recommended because it is easy to clean—just knock off the plaster after it hardens.

The mixing bucket is used to combine plaster with water; and the clean-up bucket is filled with water to clean hands and utensils. Dispose of the water outdoors or in the garbage. DO NOT WASH HANDS OR UTENSILS IN A SINK because plaster may harden in the pipes and ruin your plumbing.

A stirring utensil, used to mix plaster with water, may be a wooden spoon, plastic spoon, potato masher, etc.

Molds for plaster are made of rubber or plastic and may be purchased from hobby stores or through craft catalogs. The same molds can also be used to cast candles, plastic resin, or papier mâché.

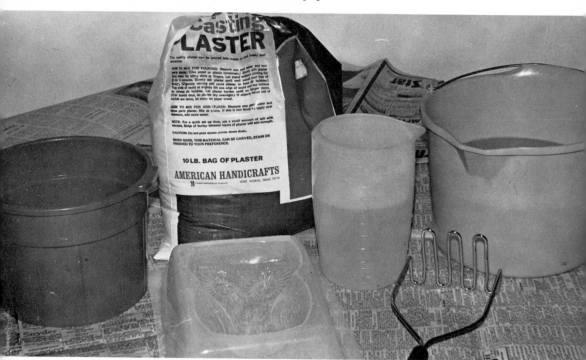

Assemble materials within easy reach. The plaster illustrated may be purchased at any American Handicrafts Company store.

Gather the above materials within handy reach from where you sit or stand. Cover the work area with newspapers or a sheet of plastic to protect the surface. Then follow these easy directions.

1. Measure the amount of plaster and water needed to fill the mold. Follow the proportion of plaster to water as given by the manufacturer. Generally this is 60 percent plaster to 40 percent water or 1½ parts plaster to 1 part water. Measure only the amount you can use within a short period of time.

(An easy way to figure proportions is to fill the mold with water, then pour the water into a large measuring cup or darkroom graduate. If the water needed equals two cups, for example, then you will need three cups of plaster. An exact measurement is not crucial because plaster hardens by a chemical reaction, not evaporation of water.)

2. Pour the water into the mixing bucket. Slowly pour or sift plaster into the center of the container until it forms a small mountain. ALWAYS ADD PLASTER TO WATER, not vice versa. Allow the plaster to settle for two or three minutes while the chemical reaction begins.

Stir plaster gently to avoid air bubbles.

3. Begin gently stirring the mixture from the bottom of the container until it is creamy smooth like buttermilk or heavy pancake batter. Gentle stirring is a must because you may otherwise cause air bubbles. Also, excessive stirring hastens the setting time. Let the stirred mixture stand for a minute or two before pouring into the mold.

Pour mixture slowly into mold.

4. Slowly pour the mixture into the mold, filling plaque molds nearly to the top and statuary molds completely full. (Statuary molds are usually in two parts which are held together with clamps or clothespins during pouring.) Shake or tap the mold to release air bubbles and to level plaster.

When using statuary molds or molds made of rubber, you may wish to use a mold release before pouring to ensure that the plaster can be removed easily when dry. You can use a commercial mold release, or simply swish the mold with a tablespoon of liquid detergent in a pint of water. When using plaque molds, you may wish to nestle the mold in sand or nail it to wooden blocks; this helps the casting be level and undistorted. Large plaques may be reduced in weight by sandwiching a filler material such as sisal or burlap between layers of plaster.

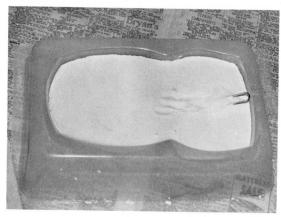

Embed rustproof hanger in plaster plaques.

5. If you are casting a plaque, embed a hanger in the plaster after it has set for about five minutes. Use plastercraft hangers, sawtooth hangers, or make your own hangers from stainless steel or brass. (Hairpins or paper clips will rust and leave discolorations on the plaque and wall.) When the plaque is large, use more than one hanger to distribute the weight when hung.

CLEAN HANDS AND UTENSILS IN CLEAN-UP BUCKET, NOT SINK.

6. Let plaster cure to room temperature. Plaster generally hardens within an hour, becoming very warm as it hardens then becoming very cool as it cures (remember, it's a chemical reaction).

Remove from mold when plaster cures to room temperature.

Casting must be completely dry before painting or paint may bubble and flake.

7. Remove plaster from mold. If the mold is plastic, simply lay it plaster-side down and gently press the center of the mold with your thumbs as your fingers lift the sides of the mold upwards—the way you remove ice cubes from a plastic tray. If the mold is rubber, peel it off starting from the bottom—like removing a rubber glove. To aid the rubber in sliding over itself, you may lubricate the outside of the mold with talcum powder, soapy water, or liquid soap. Wash molds with fresh lukewarm water before storing.

The face of the plaster will still be somewhat soft. You should let it dry completely—usually overnight—by laying it on a wire rack where the air can circulate. If needed, remove excess plaster and smooth edges and seams with a dull knife.

Thus, in a few simple steps you have created your own plaster whiteware, now ready for painting and decorating.

ORIGINAL PLASTER CASTINGS

You can cast plaster in plastic or rubber molds or you can make your own mold. You can create a casting in sand, in balloons, in egg cartons, and so forth. Plaster will take the shape of anything you pour it into, so your imagination is the limit.

Sand casting, for example, is easily accomplished in three steps:

1. Fill plastic tub or cardboard box with sand and add just enough water to make the sand pack easily. Scoop a design in the sand with your hand or a spoon. The design may be a fish, mushroom, owl, or simply a pleasing shape. You may also embed treasured objects such as agates, shells, candles, etc., in the sand cavity.

2. Pour the plaster/water mixture into the design cavity and let cure overnight. As with commercial molds, do not overfill.

3. Carefully remove plaster from sand and brush or blow off loose sand. The casting may now be complete if you like a rough, textured effect—or you may paint and decorate it. (See color section.)

Agates or other treasures are easily added to sand-casting designs.

Plaster assumes the shape of any design you create in sand.

Casting in household containers is another idea to use up leftover plaster. Use a container that you can peel or tear, or somehow separate the plaster from the container when dry. For example, you can pour plaster into egg cartons and use the shapes for mushroom caps. You can pour plaster into an aluminum pie tin and use the plaque for decoupage or tole painting. Or, while the plaster is setting up, press baby's hand or foot into the plaster for a permanent souvenir.

Plaster may be poured in household containers such as egg cartons to create interesting shapes.

Balloon casting is also a fun idea, especially for youngsters. An inflated balloon serves as a mold while your hands shape the design during the ten or fifteen minutes it takes for plaster to set up. The trick is to get the plaster into the balloon and shape the form before the plaster hardens. It's simple but messy, so be sure to first protect work area and floor with newspaper. Then:

1. Mix plaster and water, using very cold water and a minimum of stirring to slow the setting time. Pour plaster immediately into a small-necked bottle (a beverage or ketchup bottle works nicely). A funnel may be used if you have difficulty pouring directly from the mixing bucket. Working quickly, place an inflated balloon over the neck of the bottle. (Pinch balloon with one hand while fitting over bottle neck with the other hand to prevent air from escaping.) Turn the bottle upside down and plaster will flow into the balloon. Fill balloon with plaster until it contains the amount desired. Large balloons are easiest to work with.

2. Remove balloon from bottle neck, pinching the balloon to prevent air from escaping. Then slowly let excess air escape so that only plaster fills the balloon. Tie a knot in the end of the balloon so the plaster won't seep out, then let set for a few minutes.

3. Work the plaster with your hands until the desired shape is attained. Roundish shapes such as novelty worms, owls, cats, mice, fruit, etc., are easiest when casting with balloons. You may make more than one round shape by segmenting the balloon with rubber bands. Or, you may allow the plaster to settle of its own accord into a shape. When the plaster begins to feel warm, it has started to set up. Set the balloon on a level table or shelf and let cure to room temperature.

4. In about an hour, the balloon may be removed so that the casting can dry more thoroughly. Preferably the casting should dry overnight on a wire rack.

5. When completely dry, the balloon casting may be sealed and decorated as explained in the next chapter. However, these novelty shapes can also be decorated with yarn, buttons, eyelashes, sequins, and so forth. Seal, paint, then add these accents with white glue.

Pour plaster into balloons with the help of a bottle, then shape the balloons with your hands.

Paint and decorate balloon castings into the "critter" the shape most closely resembles.

Carving plaster is another exciting way to express creativity. What's more, it's easy. People who have never before attempted to carve can find themselves shaping realistic heads, totem poles, animals, and oriental gods or impressionistic free-form designs. Select a shape—perhaps using a picture to guide you. Then follow these steps:

1. Mix plaster and water, using more plaster than usual for a sturdier piece; three parts plaster to one part water is a good guide. (Before adding plaster, you can mix in other ingredients, such as coffee grounds, sand, vermiculite, etc., to give texture.) After the mixture has set for two or three minutes, pour into a container that is approximately the same size as you wish the carving to be. The container should be easily removable. Milk cartons, cottage cheese containers, and cardboard frozen juice containers are perfect.

2. Let the plaster cure to room temperature, then remove the container. You may begin carving immediately. If needed, you may draw the design on the plaster with a pencil or felt tip pen to guide you as you carve. Any sharp implement, such as pocketknife, modeling tool, linoleum cutter, drill, chisel, etc., may be used to carve. Carve plaster into the general shape desired, then add detail.

3. If you carve away more than you intend, mix more plaster and patch the area. A fresh plaster mixture may also be used to add hair, eyebrows, squiggly designs, and so forth—just dab on plaster with a toothpick.

4. Let the carving dry completely, at least overnight, before sealing and decorating. Even if paint and decorating are not desired, the carving should be sealed with lacquer sealer, clear varnish, or any art finish. This seals out moisture so that plaster will not mildew.

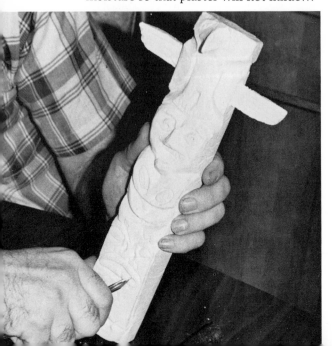

Plaster may be carved with any sharp household tool, even electric drills.

A drill or ice pick provides a simple way to add eyes to carvings.

This clever totem pole was originally cast in a waxed milk carton. After the main body was carved, wings were added with a fresh plaster mixture. Created by Keith Robinson.

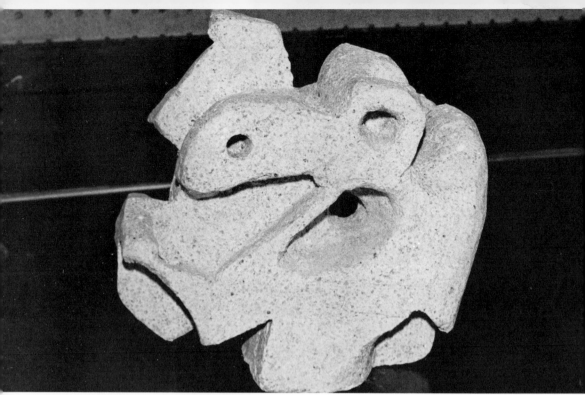

This free-form carving was given texture by adding vermiculite to plaster-water mixture. Created by Teresa Gilbert.

This novel design was carved in one evening. After drying overnight, the letters were painted in bright "mod" colors. Created by Janet Robinson.

Carving plaster is easy enough to provide youngsters with hours of fun. Flower created by Mary Robinson, age ten, free-form carving by Tina Robinson, age twelve.

Sculpting plaster is similar to carving plaster except that you build plaster up into the general shape rather than carve it down. Quite often, an armature such as a wire hanger, Styrofoam ball, paper towel core, or such, is used to help form the shape.

Because plaster hardens quickly, you would be wise to mix several batches of plaster/water (using the thicker three parts plaster to one part water ratio). This allows you to work your way from the bottom up or from the inside out. For example, if you are sculpting a figure of a man, the first mixture could be used for the base, second mixture for the legs, third batch for the torso, fourth batch for the head. The wet new plaster will adhere to the already hardened plaster.

Or, using a man's head for example, you can work your way inside out by using the first mixture to cover an armature (say a round Styrofoam ball); the second mixture could build up the head's shape more realistically; and a final batch could add plaster for ears and nose.

After the general shape is attained, you may model the final features with your hands. However, plaster hardens within ten to fifteen minutes, which seldom allows enough time to model most projects. So final details may be added with hammer and chisel, pocketknife, modeling tool, drill, and so forth.

Let the completed sculpture dry thoroughly before sealing or painting.

Another way to "sculpt" plaster is to dip gauze into the plaster water mixture, then wrap it around an armature. (Gauze with plaster already in it that only needs to be dipped in water is also available from art supply outlets.) Continue wrapping the plastered gauze around the armature until the desired shape is reached. Clever results are often obtained when you use a human for your armature: just apply a thick coating of petroleum jelly to the portion of anatomy you will be using, then apply several layers of plaster-dipped gauze. Work quickly so the plaster won't harden in the mixing pail before you are finished. Your model will feel the warmth of the plaster setting up, but within about ten minutes the plaster will be hard enough to remove. Let dry overnight before sealing or painting.

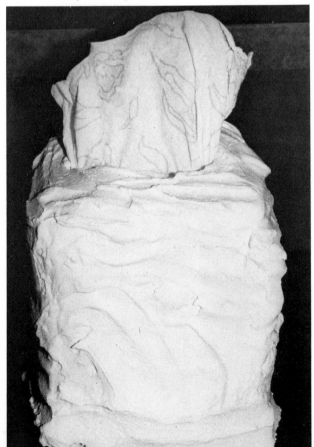

Using a cardboard tissue box as an armature, the author sculpted a practical yet decorative accent for the bathroom.

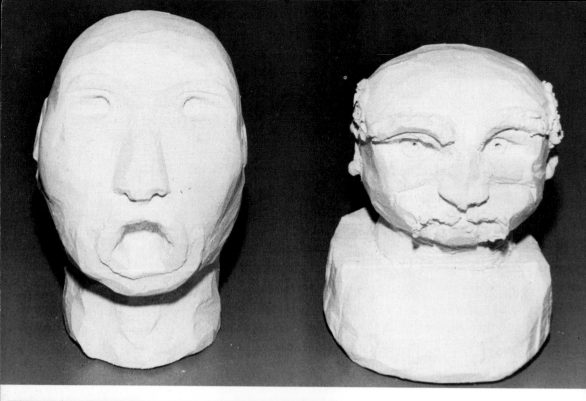

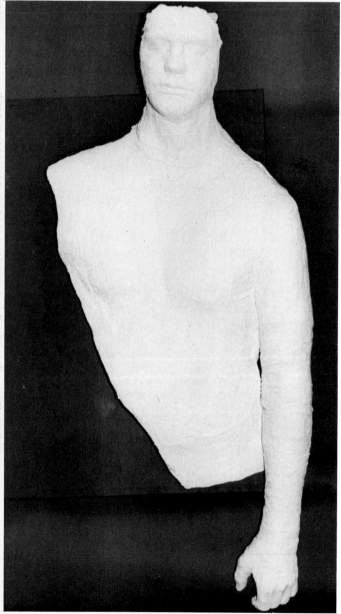

Because plaster hardens so quickly, several batches may be needed to complete a project. The ancient Indian head was created by first covering a toilet paper core. Additional batches were added until the general shape was attained, then facial features were carved. The Teddy Roosevelt head does not have an armature; it was created by using the first plaster mixture for the base, second for neck, third for head, and fourth for facial hair and nose. A pocketknife was used to add detail and smooth the shape. Created by Keith Robinson, Lavila Robinson, and Mike Van Curler.

Although human armatures can feel the warmth of the plaster as it sets up, it will not burn and the casting should be hard enough to remove in ten or fifteen minutes. Created by Randy Ransom.

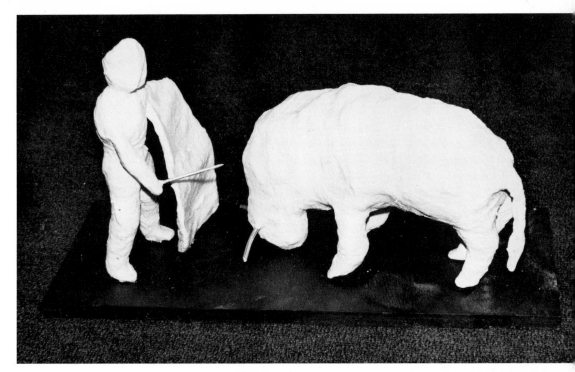

Gauze dipped in plaster was wrapped around a wire armature to obtain this clever bullfight scene. Created by Teresa Gilbert.

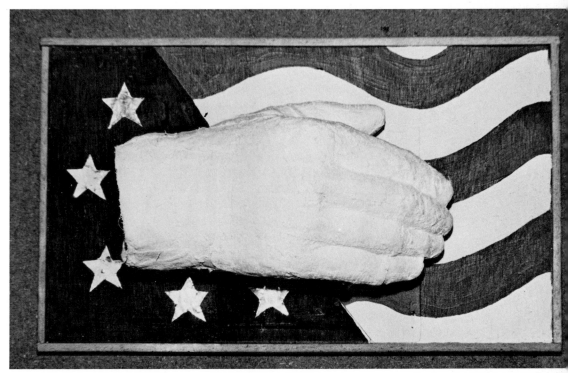

Use the human body as an armature. Coat hand with petroleum jelly and apply gauze dipped in wet plaster. Created by Randy Ransom.

3

Ready, Set ... Create

Now comes the fun of decorating the plaster whiteware you have selected. It's a great chance for self-expression because you have an endless variety of paints and finishes to choose from. The colors you select and the way you apply them will give your plastercraft a stamp of individuality.

If choosing colors leaves you in a quandary, browse through the pictures in this book for ideas. Or, look at ceramic figurines in variety stores, copy plastercraft samples in hobby stores, thumb through craft catalogs. Consider the decor of the room in which the plastercraft will be displayed. If the room has orange accent colors, then use orange on the plastercraft. Another way to choose colors is to let the plastercraft design be your guide. If the design is a famous statue, paint the plaster to simulate aged marble. If the design is a plaque of fruit on a wood background, use realistic fruit colors and a wood-color antiquing stain.

No matter how you decide to decorate plaster, you will need to invest a small amount in paints and brushes. The amount is slight—two to ten dollars —for a hobby that will bring you a lifetime of pleasure.

GETTING READY WITH MATERIALS

Let's begin with paints. Plaster whiteware is usually painted in three steps with a sealer, a base coat, and a protective finish. (An antiquing stain is often used also—see chapter 4 for further details.)

The sealer coats whiteware, which is very porous, so that the base coat colors will not be absorbed. It serves the same function on plaster that a wood sealer does on wood. Sealer may be brushed on or sprayed on. The brush-on type comes in small jars for about fifty cents, requires only one coat, and may be cleaned up with water. The spray-on type is a lacquer sealer that requires two light coats and costs about two dollars. Both types of sealer will last through several projects. If sealer is unavailable, substitute any type of art sealer or fixative, clear varnish, white paint, or a protective finish.

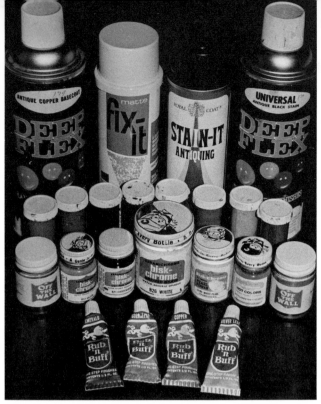

An excellent variety of paints suitable for plastercraft enables every project to have a stamp of individuality.

The base coat is what gives plastercraft its color. Although almost any type of paint may be used for the base coat, most people prefer acrylic craft paints for hand painting plaster. These paints are bottled in small jars in every color of the rainbow. The label should state that the paint is suitable for plaster or fired ceramic (often wood, metal, glass, and paper as well).

Acrylic craft paints are popular because they dry within ten to twenty minutes and because they are water soluble. Brushes and hands are easily cleaned with soap and water.

Select the colors needed to complete your plaster design. For example, if you are painting a figurine, you should select colors for flesh, eyes, hair, clothes, and so forth. A basic selection of colors would include:

white	red	tan
black	blue	yellow
brown	green	flesh

These colors may be mixed to create many other colors. For instance, mix yellow and red to get orange. Mix white and black to get gray. Mix green and yellow to get bright lime green. Mix red and blue to get purple. If you are a beginner, however, it will be easier to purchase all needed colors already mixed, such as turquoise, olive green, hot pink, etc. If you do mix colors, mix an ample amount in case a second coat or touch-up is needed.

Because acrylic paints dry quickly when exposed to air, keep the jars tightly sealed when not in use. Wipe the cap and mouth of jar before sealing to prevent sticking. Stubborn lids may be loosened by holding under hot tap water.

A protective finish is used after the base coat has dried to protect the piece from handling and fading. Any type of spray-on craft finish, sealer, or fixative (or even clear varnish) may be used. There are excellent handiwork finishes on the market that can enhance plastercraft by adding a high gloss, a matte finish, or even an iridescent pearl sheen.

Four soft-bristled watercolor brushes will fill most hand-painting needs.

Brushes for plastercraft can be almost any type you already have on hand. If you need new brushes, however, short soft-bristled watercolor brushes are most satisfactory. A selection of four different size brushes should be adequate:

a medium size (#5 or #6) round-tipped brush
a small size (#1 or #2) round-tipped brush
a medium size (#5 to #8) flat-edged brush
a large (½ inch) flat-edged brush

Expensive brushes are not necessary, but do avoid "cheapies." Bargain brushes often lose their bristles, are difficult to control, and do not keep a nice point or edge. When bristles do go awry, pull out the wayward bristle or trim with scissors.

With care, brushes will last through many projects. Never allow paint to dry in the brush: clean in water between colors and wash immediately with soap and cool water when finished. Store with bristles up or flat so they will not bend out of shape.

A work area. Supplies found in the home will complete your plastercraft needs. A kitchen table with sturdy legs is ideal for a work area. Cover the table with newspaper to protect it from paint. Good lighting is important. Move the table or add a lamp so that you can see without shadows.

Baby food or mustard jars are perfect for holding water used to clean brushes between colors. Keep old rags or a box of paper tissues handy to wipe water out of brushes and to clean any paint that gets on your hands.

And that's all there is to getting ready for plastercraft.

GETTING SET—CLEAN AND SEAL

Most often plaster whiteware is completely ready for you to apply the sealer. But sometimes whiteware is a bit dirty, has an unwanted nubbin or two, or maybe a hole or chip.

That's no problem. Plaster castings are easily cleaned and repaired in seconds.

Cleaning whiteware. The simplest way to clean dust off whiteware is to blow it off. If you're a bit timid about using your own breath, use a rubber blower. Or brush the entire piece with a clean dry paintbrush. Or dust with a soft lintless rag. Avoid dusting with your hand—body oil may be transferred to the whiteware.

Sometimes plaster whiteware is wrapped in newspaper at the store, which leaves newsprint marks, or maybe the price is written in pencil. Use a moist synthetic sponge (foam rubber or Polyfoam) to gently rub off such marks. Don't rub too hard, though, or you'll also remove the plaster.

Cleaning takes seconds but is a very important step. Any dust allowed to remain will increase in size as it is coated with paint. Newsprint can be covered with dark paint but will show through light-colored paints. Any stain or dirt allowed to remain will not magically disappear, but will stay around to haunt the finished appearance of your plastercraft. So get rid of it first.

A rubber blower or dry paintbrush can remove dust and dirt.

Wipe away smudges with a moist synthetic sponge.

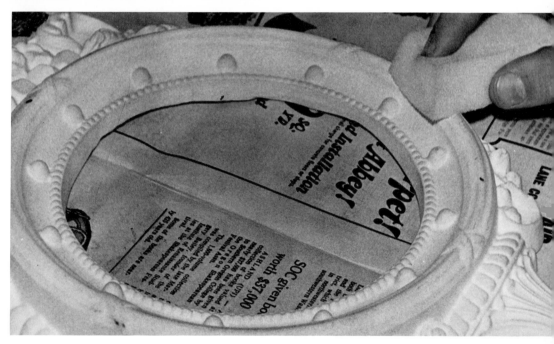

Easy repairs. When you select plaster whiteware, try to find castings that are free of chips, holes, or nubbins. However, these defects are easily repaired if you have no choice.

Repair chips and holes with a spackling paste available at hardware and variety stores. Remove all loose, scaly, or powdery material around the chip or hole. Then apply spackling paste with a small wooden stick or your finger. Completely fill and cover the defective area with paste. Then shape it and smooth it into the plaster with a clean finger. This compound dries quickly and you should be able to seal the plaster within half an hour after using spackling paste.

Rough or grainy areas are also easily repaired. Sand the area with an emery board, fingernail file, small-grained sandpaper, or a moist synthetic sponge. Go slowly and carefully, especially with a sponge, or you can rub away more than you intend.

When tiny plaster nubbins or bumps are stuck on whiteware, remove them with your fingernail, a modeling tool, or the wooden end of a paintbrush. Use slight pressure to pry the nubbin loose.

23

Repair chips and holes with spackling paste.

Remove unwanted lumps and nubbins with a modeling tool or fingernail.

If a piece of the casting should break off, you may glue clean, dry plaster with white glue such as Elmer's or white craft glue.

Sealing whiteware. While you are sealing the plaster is a good time to start planning the design of the finished piece. As you apply the sealer, you can study the design to decide which colors you are going to use, in what order you wish to paint, and which protective finish will best suit the design.

It was mentioned earlier that you have a choice of brush-on sealer or spray-on sealer. When using brush-on sealer, stir or shake the jar, then apply liberally with a large flat-edged brush. (Shaking the jar causes more bubbles than stirring.) For best results, plaster and sealer should be at room temperature.

Apply sealer liberally, painting one definite area at a time.

Properly sealed whiteware results in a more professional-looking piece. Aztec sun god design painted by Kelly McCurdy.

Paint your way from top to bottom or from one area to another. Because the sealer is often the same color as whiteware, it may be difficult to be sure you have completely covered the whiteware unless you work from one definite area to another.

Aim for a smooth, evenly applied coat. Use the brush to work out any tiny air bubbles that occur as you paint. And use the brush to smooth out any paint that clogs in cracks and crevices. The smoothest coat will be obtained by painting flat areas in up-and-down motions and dimensional areas in the direction of the design.

If the brush becomes stiff, dip it in water to loosen the bristles. Or add a few drops of water to thin the sealer and stir again. (Sealer may also be dabbed on with a synthetic sponge instead of a brush, but sponging causes more air bubbles than brushing.)

Within ten to fifteen minutes, the sealer will lose its gloss, which means that it is dry and you can start painting the base coat.

Applying spray-on lacquer sealer is also easy. Spread newspaper under the whiteware in a well-ventilated room (open a window). Again, sealer and plaster should be at room temperature. Mix the sealer by shaking the can for at least thirty seconds—most products have an agitator ball that should rattle during this time.

Then spray two light coats. As you spray, hold the can eight to twelve inches from the whiteware. Work your way from top to bottom to make sure the whiteware is completely covered, including edges. Let the first coat dry at least twenty minutes. When dry to touch, apply the second coat. Two light coats are recommended rather than one heavy coat to prevent running, paint build-up in cracks, and more thorough coverage (you might miss a spot during the first coat but you would cover it with the second coat).

After the second coat has dried, you may begin to paint the base coat.

May the sealer ever be omitted? No, although you may substitute clear varnish, white paint, an art fixative, or protective finish for the lacquer sealer. Plaster is porous and will absorb the base coat too quickly if you omit the sealing step. By applying sealer, you will have an easier time brushing on colors; it will take less paint and fewer coats to color whiteware; and the protective finish will settle more evenly.

Thus, cleaning, repairing, and sealing whiteware are all essential steps leading to professional-looking plastercraft art.

CREATING THE FIRST PROJECT

Normally cleaning and sealing plaster whiteware takes less than half an hour. So within a very short time you'll be ready for one of the most enjoyable aspects of plastercraft—creating color. (Remember, paints and plaster should always be at room temperature to create color instead of chaos.)

Applying the base coat. Where do you begin? The answer depends upon the design you are painting and the base-coat colors you are using. The ultimate goal, of course, is to follow the design exactly without slopping paint where it's not wanted. Unless you have an extremely steady hand, you will probably make mistakes on your first few projects. But you can cover mistakes as you paint by following these guidelines:

1. Paint light colors first. If you should make a mistake with a light color, it will be covered when you paint a darker color over it.

2. Paint from top to bottom. By painting your way downward, you eliminate the possibility of smearing or smudging painted areas with your hand. If you do get paint on your hand, wash it off.

3. Paint difficult areas first. For example, if a figure looks difficult to paint and you think you may "slop" paint into adjoining areas, then paint the hard part first. That way you can cover mistakes when you reach the easier part.

4. Paint backgrounds first. It is easier to paint the background, then cover any mistakes while painting the foreground.

Obviously you can't paint everything first all the time. With these guidelines in mind, however, you can formulate a plan of attack to help you paint in a logical progression.

After you have decided upon a painting sequence, start painting. And here are the Top Ten Tips to ensure that your first project will be a success:

Top Ten Tips

1. The best way to eliminate mistakes is to master control of your brush so that it never swerves into the wrong area. Hold the brush tightly with thumb, first and second fingers around the ferrule (the metal part). Brace the edge of your hand or your little finger on the whiteware; the rest of your hand thus serves as a pivot point as you swing the brush.

2. Turn the whiteware so that you can always reach the spot you are painting as easily as possible. Hold the whiteware in your lap or tilt it up on the table. Try painting plaques on a lazy Susan so that turning is easier. Or move yourself around to reach every spot. Remember, the better you can get at the area you are painting, the better job you can do.

3. Select brushes that best fit the area you are painting. A large flat brush will work nicely for the background, but perhaps you should switch to a smaller round brush when painting the backround area that adjoins the fore-

ground. When in doubt about which brush to use, always choose the smaller. In time, you'll develop definite preferences about which brush to use when.

4. Follow the shape of the design as you paint. For example, flower petals grow from the center outwards, so paint from the center to the edge. If a vine or stem curves, then swing the brush to follow the curve. When there is no definite shape to follow, always paint vertically in up-and-down motions. By painting consistently in the same direction, the color will look smoother when dry; the plaster will be easier to cover; and you avoid any runny buildup of color in crevices.

5. Always smooth out air bubbles. Pull the brush over bubbles in the paint until they disappear. If bubbles are not smoothed out, they will chip and crack when dry. Likewise, smooth out paint that clogs in cracks and crevices.

6. Allow each color to dry before painting adjoining colors. Depending upon the paint and temperature of the room, acrylic craft paint will dry in ten to twenty minutes. When dry, it will lose its shine. Test by touching lightly. The reason for waiting is that the old color may smear or become gummy if it is not dry when the new color touches it.

7. Keep paint flowing. Midway through the painting session, you may notice that the paint becomes more difficult to brush on. This is because acrylic paint dries very quickly—in its jar and on your brush. So when the paint no longer flows easily off your brush, you should thin it with a few drops of water. Stir to blend (shaking causes bubbles). When paint has dried in the brush, dip the brush in water, swish it clean, and wipe with a tissue or rag to remove excess moisture. To prevent drying, keep paint jars tightly sealed when you are not using them. And clean brushes in water immediately—even if you are only taking a coffee break.

8. As you paint, be on your guard for cleanliness. Wash or wipe any paint off your hands; otherwise you're apt to transfer paint from your hands to the whiteware. Clean brushes well whenever changing colors. A lingering bit of yellow in the brush, for instance, will turn your blue into green. And watch for bristles and dust that lodge themselves in the drying paint. Remove with fingers or tweezers.

9. Use two coats of paint if needed. Although one coat of paint will often do the job, use another coat if the color looks runny, streaked, or white shows through. Paint quality varies from brand to brand, so if a color requires more than two coats, try switching brands.

10. Use white paint as an erasure. When paint is deposited in an unwanted area, light colors can easily be covered with a darker color. But, if the unwanted paint is a dark color that cannot be covered, then paint the dark color white. When dry, apply the color you want over the white paint.

But the most important tip of all hasn't been mentioned. And that is: Relax! Painting whiteware is fun. It's one of the most creative steps of plastercraft. So take your time and enjoy it.

Before you begin, plan a painting sequence that hides mistakes as you paint.

Hold brush tightly near bristles and brace your little finger on whiteware for better control of brush.

Tilt, tip, and turn whiteware to reach hard-to-get-at areas.

Pull brush in the same direction as the design.

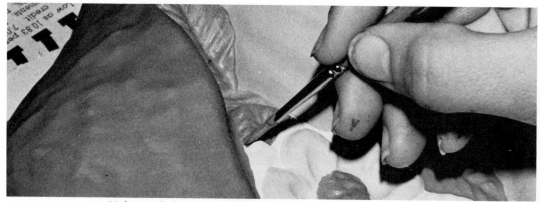

Hide wiggly lines by painting darker colors over lighter colors.

Applying the protective finish. Your plastercraft won't be complete until you protect it from the ravages of time. This is easily accomplished by spraying on a protective finish that prevents the paint from dulling and coats it so that dirt and dust can be removed with a damp cloth.

But protective finishes can do much more than just protect. A wide selection of handicraft finishes and spray varnishes are available to enhance your work. A normal gloss finish, for example, gives plaster a nicely hand-polished sheen. A high gloss or plastic finish makes plaster look like a shiny fired ceramic. A matte or bisque finish dulls the base coat into a delicate age-old look. And pearlized finishes give colors an iridescent twinkle.

Because protective finishes are contained in spray cans, they are easy to apply in five simple steps. The instructions for their use should be followed when any type of spray paint is used, such as spray-on colors, "metal look" sprays, glass staining sprays, and spray-on antiquing stain.

1. Be sure plaster is clean and dry. Acrylic base coats should be allowed to cure at least an hour and preferably overnight. (Chances of paint chipping or cracking are increased when the drying time is rushed.) Use a soft dry brush or lintless rag to remove any lint or dust.

2. Prepare a work area. Spray paints and finishes should be used in a well-ventilated area that will not be damaged by stray paint. Spread newspaper on garage or patio floors, for example. (Spray outdoors only when weather is temperate so plaster and paint will remain at room temperature.) If spraying indoors, open a window and place the plaster inside a cardboard box so that stray paint will not damage walls or floors.

3. Shake the can to mix according to manufacturer's instructions. Often an agitator ball should rattle as you shake for at least thirty seconds. The can should be at room temperature (68 to 72 degrees). If not, place in warm water for five to ten minutes before shaking.

4. Spray the first light coat. Hold the can approximately 8 to 12 inches from the surface while spraying. Use even, overlapping strokes. Move around the plastercraft or use a turntable (or old piano stool) to ensure that the entire surface is coated, including edges. Let dry about twenty minutes (or according to manufacturer's instructions) until dry to touch, then apply a second coat. Two light coats are superior to one heavy coat because a heavy coat will run, build up in cracks, and may not cover completely. Use additional coats, if desired, for a more satiny effect with low gloss and matte finishes—for a shiny ceramic effect with normal and high gloss finishes.

5. When finished, clean the spray head of the can by turning upside down and depressing for three seconds or until paint no longer comes out. This keeps the head from clogging, so it will last through many plastercraft projects.

This protective finish will last a lifetime of normal use. However, if you plan to display the plaster outdoors, you may wish to give it additional coats of plastic varnish for weatherproofing.

That's all there is to it. Your first plastercraft project is now complete (unless you wish to mellow colors and add rich shading by antiquing). Within a few hours, you've turned an uncolored plaster casting into a hand-painted object of beauty.

A high-gloss protective finish gives this mushroom bouquet the appearance of shiny fired ceramic.

4

Antiquing Makes a Difference

You'll notice that some plastercraft looks so-so and other plaster art really has oomph. The difference is often made by antiquing. An antiquing stain adds shading to cracks and crevices, mellows bright colors, and gives most pieces a rich professional look.

Fortunately, antiquing is a simple process that requires only about a half hour's time to do. So, if you want to add oomph to your plastercraft, here's how.

BASIC ANTIQUING

Only three items are required to antique. First, you'll need an antiquing stain (or glaze) available in small jars or spray cans from the hobby store. For most projects, a walnut, fruitwood, or burnt umber stain works nicely. Or, mix your own stain with one part burnt umber artists' oil and one part paint thinner or turpentine. Second, you'll need a soft lintless rag, old nylon stocking, cheesecloth, or a piece of synthetic sponge (foam rubber or Polyfoam) to wipe the stain. Paper tissue may also be used, but it sometimes leaves lint embedded in the stain. Last, you'll need a soft-bristled brush, about one inch wide, to distribute the stain smoothly and evenly. The brush may be larger or smaller, depending upon the size of the piece you are antiquing.

If you have completed the base coat and protective finish, as explained in the last chapter, you are now ready to antique. *Two light coats of a protective finish are required over acrylic before antiquing.* Without this protection, acrylic paints may become streaky or crumbly during antiquing.

Again, both plaster and stain should be at room temperature. Spread newspapers over the work area to protect tabletops from antiquing stain—it's messy. And, if you're using a spray stain, you should place the plaster in a cardboard box to confine the spray to the object instead of your walls. Let's begin:

1. Spray or brush on the stain. It should completely cover every nook and cranny of your pastercraft, including edges, so that the whole piece looks

brown. Let the stain dry until it begins to lose its gloss. Drying time may be from two to twenty minutes, depending upon the stain, so read the manufacturer's instructions carefully.

2. Gently wipe the stain with rag, tissue, old nylon, cheesecloth, or foam rubber when the stain begins to lose its gloss. (Foam rubber is a favorite because it is most absorbent.) Wipe from top to bottom. Because plaster whiteware is three-dimensional, this gentle wiping will remove stain from protruding areas but leave it in cracks and crevices—thus giving a naturally aged look. Remove as much or as little stain as desired. Use clean tissues or find clean areas on the rag or foam rubber as it becomes muddy with stain. Unless you wipe with a clean material, you'll be transferring stain from one area to another instead of removing it.

3. After wiping off as much stain as desired, use the soft dry brush to pull the remaining stain from top to bottom and to shade where desired. This brushing step is a secret that many plastercraft artists overlook. But brushing distributes the stain more evenly, gives a woodgrain effect, and prevents that dirty look that sometimes results when stain clogs in crevices. Wipe the brush clean on newspaper or rags after every few strokes.

Now step back and inspect your antiquing job. If too much stain still remains, wipe or brush more off. If you've removed too much stain, you can often dab stain back on, using the dirty rag or foam rubber—or use the brush to borrow extra stain from a crevice to apply elsewhere. Sometimes spray-on stain will begin to dry before you are through antiquing. If this happens, use paint thinner (or water if the stain is acrylic) to make the stain workable again. Or, spray on more stain, which also tends to loosen the original stain.

4. Let the stain dry at least two hours and preferably overnight at room temperature in a dust-free place where people won't touch it. When the stain is completely dry, protect it with two or more light coats of protective finish, as explained in the last chapter. A low gloss or matte finish is most compatible with the antique look.

Finally, admire your work—for antiquing certainly makes a world of difference. Without antiquing, plastercraft looks like a cute novelty from the dime store. With antiquing, it looks like a work of art from an exclusive gift shop.

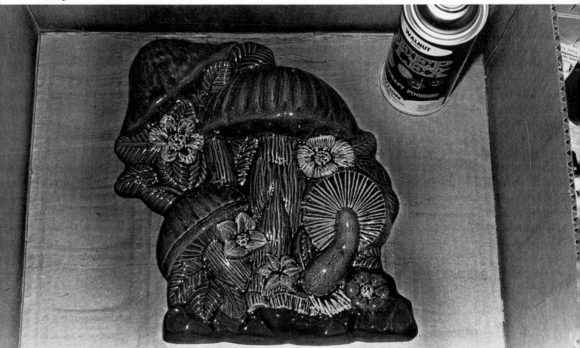

Spray or brush on antiquing stain until plaster is completely covered.

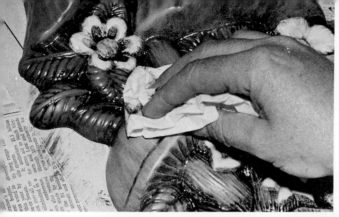

Wipe plaster gently to remove excess stain, allowing stain to remain in cracks and crevices.

Pull a dry brush from top to bottom for the ultimate in a rich, professional look.

After stain cures overnight, add a protective finish and admire! (Make a "before and after" comparison with the plaque pictured on page 32)

"WOOD LOOK" ANTIQUING

"Wood look" antiquing can not only transform plain plaster into rich carved wood, but this method also allows you to omit a few steps by using spray enamel paints rather than brush-on acrylic craft colors.

Under BASIC ANTIQUING, it was assumed that you used acrylic craft paints, which require a protective coating before applying antiquing stain. You also had to let adjoining acrylic colors dry before adding the next color. With "wood look" antiquing, however, you only need one color for a base coat, so it will save time to use a spray enamel or oil-base paint that does not require a protective coating before antiquing. Suggested colors are tan, nutmeg, cocoa, woodtone, etc. Avoid dark brown because the stain will not show up well on a dark base coat. Thus, you simply seal, spray two light enamel base coats, apply antiquing stain, and finish with a protective coating. More specifically:

1. Seal plaster as usual. If spray enamel is used, it may be substituted as a sealer.

2. Apply a base coat, using a light or medium brown color. If an acrylic base coat is used, seal with a protective finish before the next step. If spray enamel is used, apply two light coats following manufacturer's instructions or refer to spraying instructions given in chapter 3 under *Applying the protective finish*. Be sure paints are completely dry before proceeding to next step.

3. Apply a wood color antiquing stain, such as walnut, burnt umber, fruitwood, etc. Wipe and brush the stain as explained under BASIC ANTIQUING. Brushing is especially important to obtain a "wood" look because brushing from top to bottom (always pull the brush in the same direction) gives a wood-grain effect. If the design has a horizontal wood grain, then pull the brush from side to side. If a rough, weathered wood look is desired, use a hard-bristled instead of soft-bristled dry brush.

4. After the stain has dried two hours or preferably overnight (read manufacturer's instructions), give the piece two or more coats of a protective finish. A low or normal gloss finish gives plaster the look of hand-waxed wood, while a matte or bisque finish gives plaster a more realistic, aged look.

When you wish to create the look of painted wood, use a bright color for the base coat instead of a wood color. Spray-on enamels are easiest to use. Orange, red, olive green, and mustard yellow are especially effective base-coat colors for the painted wood effect.

Plaster plaques often have a multicolored design on a wood background. When this is the case, you are advised to use acrylic craft paints for both the background and the design. Paint the background first, using a light or medium woodtone color, then paint the design in colors of your choice. (You may use a spray enamel for the wood background, then paint the design in acrylic craft paints, but the result is not always satisfactory because acrylic paints sometimes "bead" on the slick enamel.)

After adding a protective finish, antique the whole plaque in a wood-color stain, such as walnut. Leave more stain on the wood background and less stain on the multicolored foreground. Seal with a low gloss or matte finish. Presto— the background looks exactly like carved wood and the colored design is richly shaded.

To imitate the look of wood, first apply a base coat in a light or medium brown color.

Cover the entire piece with a wood-color antiquing stain such as walnut or fruitwood.

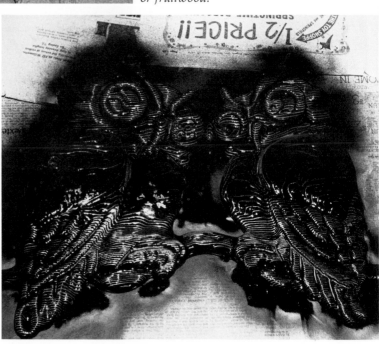

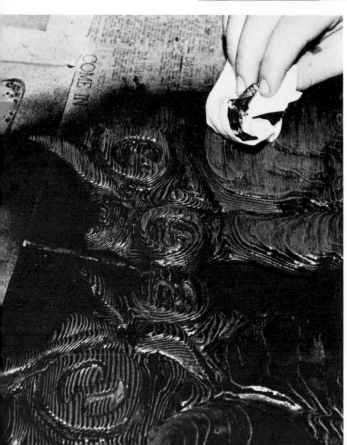

Remove excess stain, then brush following the grain.

When completed, you'll vow the piece is hand-carved wood instead of plaster.

When plaques have wooden backgrounds, apply a light or medium wood color on the background, then paint foreground in a variety of colors. Antiquing will blend the piece together. Courtesy Off the Wall of Eugene, Ore.

35

If a painted wood effect is desired, select a bright-colored base coat and antique with a wood-color stain. Courtesy Custom Arts, Eugene, Ore.

"METAL LOOK" ANTIQUING

You can easily turn plaster into gold, silver, bronze, copper, and iron by using techniques you already know. "Metal look" antiquing is easy to do in three steps, and the results are stunning.

Select a plaster design that lends itself to the metal look, such as antique keys, conquistadores, statuary busts, the federal eagle, collectors' coins, picture frames, etc. Then select base coat and stain colors that are compatible with the design. For example, a bronze base coat would be used on a statuary bust, a copper base coat on pennies, a silver base coat on Spanish armor, a gold base coat on the federal eagle, etc. A universal (black) antiquing stain resembles aged metal more closely than a wood-color stain, although walnut stain gives warm tones to gold base coats. A moss-green or patina stain will give more of an oxidized metal effect, like copper or brass that has been exposed to weather. Consult the COMPLETE ANTIQUING GUIDE in the next section for more ideas.

(For best results, select a base coat and stain in the same brand and preferably a brand intended for use on plaster, fired ceramic, or other crafts. Because paint ingredients vary, a stain in one brand may cause a base coat in another brand to bubble—especially in metal colors.)

Now, back to those three easy steps:

1. After sealing, apply the metal-colored base coat. Most metallic colors come in spray cans and are oil based, which means you do not need to add a protective finish before antiquing. Two or more light coats of base-coat spray are superior to one heavy coat.

2. When the base coat has dried, apply the antiquing stain and wipe as explained under BASIC ANTIQUING. Use a dry brush to smooth the stain. Since you are trying to duplicate the look of aged metal, leave more stain in cracks and crevices that would naturally be darker and remove more stain in protruding areas that would be lighter due to handling and exposure through the years.

3. Let stain cure at least two hours and preferably overnight, then protect with two coats of low gloss or matte finish. (High gloss tends to cheapen the effect.)

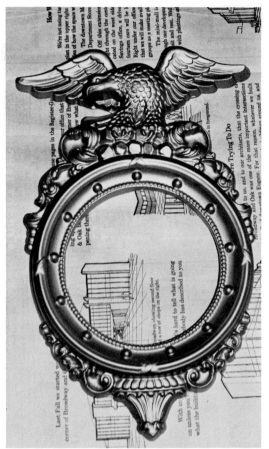

Seal and apply a metal-colored base coat.

Liberally cover with antiquing stain— usually universal (black) or moss green.

Use a dry brush to smooth stain.

Remove excess stain with rag, tissue, or foam rubber.

It's surprisingly easy to transform plaster into an "aged metal" masterpiece.

This bronze bust is an example of the many exciting finishes you can achieve by combining base coat and antiquing stain colors. Courtesy Off the Wall of Eugene, Ore.

COMPLETE ANTIQUING GUIDE

Experimenting with different color combinations in base coat and antiquing stain is fun and creative. In addition to simulating wood and metal, you can also duplicate leather, carved ivory, even Wedgwood—just by selecting the right combination of base coat and stain colors.

Although a darker stain is usually used over a lighter-colored base coat, you can reverse the process for interesting effects. As an example, you can use a dark-colored base coat such as flat black and a light-colored stain such as antique white. The result is "aged iron." Or, you can use a violet base coat and antique white stain to make "sugared grapes."

The possibilities are endless. Experiment all you like, but do aim for contrast: the antiquing stain should always be considerably darker or lighter than the base coat in order for the stain to stand out. If the experiment flops, the mistake is easily remedied. Apply another base coat and start over.

Use the following chart to guide you through any antiquing experiment in four easy steps: 1) seal; 2) apply base coat—if base coat is acrylic, protect with a spray finish; 3) antique plaster with stain or glaze; and 4) seal with a protective finish, usually low gloss or matte.

Complete Antiquing Guide*

EFFECT DESIRED	BASE COAT TO USE	STAIN TO USE
aged iron	flat black	antique white
antique bronze	antique bronze	moss green or universal
antique copper	antique copper	moss green or universal
antique gold	antique gold	moss green, walnut, or universal
antique green	olive or antique green	walnut or universal
antique red	antique red	universal
antique turquoise	jade (blue-green)	walnut or universal
antique white	antique white	antique white
bamboo	oriental bamboo (light tan)	patina or moss green
blue dusk	antique blue	antique white
burnt orange	orange	universal
carved marble	antique white	universal
creme	lemon	walnut
dusty rose	blush pink	antique white or walnut
Empire blue	antique blue	dark fruitwood or universal
fruitwood	nutmeg or woodtone	dark fruitwood
gold leaf	gold leaf	universal
Indian ivory	ivory	walnut
ivory	snow white	walnut
ivory black	flat black	pearl luster or pearl finish
leather	antique yellow	dark fruitwood
limed oak	ivory	moss green
old brick, red	red	antique white
old brick, adobe	ivory or tan	walnut or burnt umber
pumice stone	snow white	universal
silver leaf	silver leaf	universal
sugared grape	violet	antique white
teakwood	cocoa	dark fruitwood
walnut	nutmeg, wood tone	walnut
Wedgwood	periwinkle (sky blue)	antique white

* This chart is based partially upon products manufactured by Deep Flex Plastic Molds, Inc., Fort Worth, Texas. However, it is an excellent guide for all types of antiquing. If you are using other brands, select a color that closely resembles the color given on the chart.

5

Special Techniques for Plastercraft

You've already learned how to transform plaster whiteware into a hand-painted treasure, a relic of hand-carved wood, and a metal heirloom. But it's only the beginning. With the wide choice of craft paints and materials on the market, you can also transform plaster into glass, pearl, gold, velvet, and much more. Nearly any finish your imagination desires is possible.

To give full rein to your imagination, this chapter gives complete instructions for the most popular special techniques used on plastercraft.

GLASS STAINING

All it takes to turn plaster into glass is a few cans of spray paint and a few minutes. The paint is actually a bright, transparent stain that may be called a spray dye, Tiffany glass, etc. Make sure the product you buy is suitable for plaster or fired ceramic. Few colors are needed because you can create new colors as you paint.

Glass staining is a particularly effective technique on fruit, flower, and religious designs. Select a design and follow these four easy steps.

1. Seal plaster, then apply two light coats of a metallic-colored base coat. A metallic base coat is recommended because glass stains are transparent —the base coat will shimmer through the glass stain. Gold is the favorite base coat, but silver and copper are also effective.

2. When the base coat is dry, spray glass stain, using several light coats or one heavy coat. The lighter you spray, the more the base-coat color will show through. Although a heavy coat will nearly hide the base coat and cause paint buildup in crevices, this can still be an interesting effect with glass stains.

If you are using more than one color, spray the lightest color first. You may cover areas you don't want sprayed with newspaper and masking tape. However, areas where colors are allowed to overlap are intriguing. For example, if you spray flowers with an amber stain and leaves with an emerald stain, the colors will mingle into a beautiful yellow-green where they overlap. Likewise, overlapping blue and green stains will merge into a stunning aquamarine.

3. Continue spraying color after color, working your way from light colors to dark colors. For instance, use yellow, then green, then brown. You do not need to wait for one color to dry before adding another if you want the colors to overlap. Also, you can change the colors completely by adding one color on top of another wet color. In addition to creating yellow-green and aquamarine (as explained in Step 2), you can mix yellow and red to create orange; red and blue to create purple; yellow and blue to create green. In fact, creating colors as you spray is half the fun.

4. After all colors have been sprayed, you can shade the object with a brownish or root-beer-colored stain or dye. The dark stain diminishes the "sparkling glass" look a bit, but it does give a richer finish with more depth. The dark stain may also be sprayed when the other paints are wet. (If you wish to wipe or brush the dark stain, as in the antiquing process, spray the stain *after* the other colors have dried.)

With most glass-staining products you will not need to add a protective finish because the stain is permanent.

And that's how easy it is to change heavy white plaster into a delicate-looking piece of Tiffany glass.

Cover plaster with a metal-colored base coat, then spray transparent glass stains beginning with the lightest color.

Glass staining is not only a stunning technique, but also allows you to create colors as you spray.

IMITATING MOTHER-OF-PEARL

To add an iridescent sheen to plastercraft, brush on pearlized paints or spray on a pearl finish.

For example, you can purchase pearlized acrylic craft paint in assorted tints and hand paint as usual. Or, paint plaster with any type of base coat and spray on a pearl finish. This finish not only transforms ordinary colors into iridescent colors, but also serves as a protective coating.

Do use care, however, in selecting a design to be pearlized. Little plaques, dainty birds and fish, intricate picture frames, fragile flowers, religious figurines, and so forth lend themselves well to delicate pearl tints.

Pearl paints and finishes are so beautiful that friends will think you've actually ground the inner layer of a pearl oyster shell to attain the realistic effect.

Imitating mother-of-pearl is easy when you brush on delicate tints of acrylic pearl paints. Painted by Peggy Ritter.

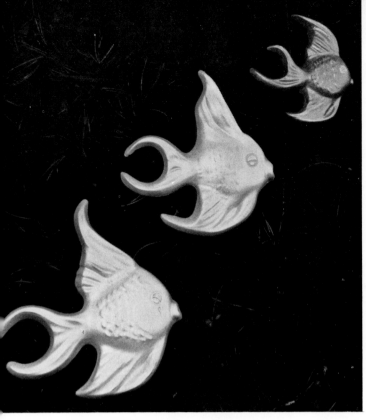

A pearl finish, sprayed on over any type of base coat, not only adds iridescent sheen but also serves as a protective coating. Painted by Janet Robinson.

ADDING METAL AND JEWEL HIGHLIGHTS

Gold, silver, copper, bronze—even jewel emerald, ruby, amethyst, and sapphire—can shimmer from your plastercraft with the aid of rub-on waxes. (These colors are actually made with pure metals or selected pigments and fine wax.) Available at hobby stores and craft centers, rub-on waxes with metallic or jewel-like sheen come in small tubes, compacts, or jars.

Easily applied with your little finger, Q-tip, or brush, wax highlights add elegance to oriental designs, Mediterranean designs, and to any design that would normally be metal—such as gun barrels, necklaces and crowns, armor and swords, antique automobiles, etc.

Although step-by-step instructions follow, you can use metal and jewel highlights anytime—but remember that these highlights are always the last coloring step. In other words, you must seal plaster, apply a base coat and antiquing (optional) *before* using metal and jewel highlights.

1. Seal plaster, then apply the base coat. If the base coat is one color only, use a spray enamel or oil-base color—this eliminates the need for a protective coating before applying the wax highlight.

Select a base-coat that will complement the highlight. For example, ebony, chocolate, or snow white provide a nicely contrasting background for bright metal colors. Or select a base-coat color that will harmonize with jewels, such as a mint green base coat with an emerald highlight; an aquamarine base coat with an amethyst highlight, and so forth. Or, go wild— use a bright orange base coat with a Grecian gold highlight; a shocking pink base coat with a ruby red highlight!

If you are using acrylic craft paints for your base-coat color, paint everything as usual including the area that will later be highlighted. Add a protective finish; antique (optional) and add another protective coating; then proceed to the next step.

2. Apply the wax directly from the tube or jar with your little finger. Use a small amount and a very gentle touch—this allows the highlight to adhere to relief areas only without filling in cracks and crevices. Steady your finger by bracing your hand on the object. If you use more than one highlight color, clean your finger with paint thinner or turpentine between colors. If you should accidentally rub highlight where it is not wanted, clean it off with a Q-tip dunked in paint thinner or turpentine.

3. When painting large areas (or using a wax for the base coat), you may wish to use a brush. If so, you may need to thin the wax color with paint thinner or turpentine. Mix in a lid or small jar. Clean brush between colors.

4. After the wax highlight has dried, some brands may be buffed with a lintless rag for added brilliance. Always protect waxes with a spray-on protective finish or clear sealer to prevent tarnishing.

After sealing and applying a base coat, rub on metal waxes with your little finger.

Large areas may be brush painted by thinning highlight color with turpentine.

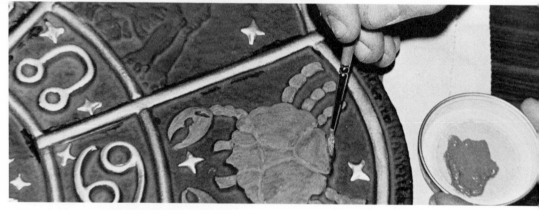

Metal and jewel highlights add luster and brilliance to plastercraft designs.

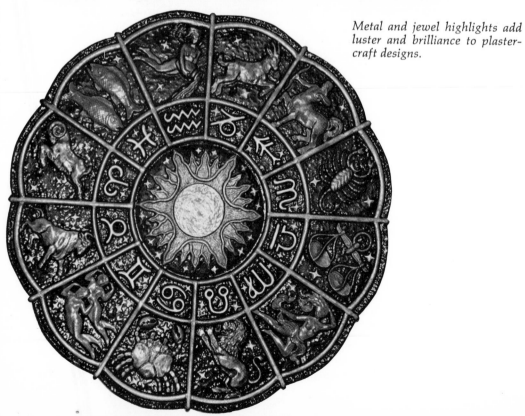

Metallic highlights, such as the gold accents on Early American spoon and fork (see color section), are added after the base coat and antiquing steps are complete.

Rub-on waxes that sparkle like jewels transformed the beehive headdress of this oriental dancer into a work of art. Courtesy Plast-a-Craft, Inc., Portland, Ore.

ANTIQUING IN REVERSE

In addition to using metal and jewel waxes to achieve lush highlights, you can also use these paints to create a rich antique effect by reversing the normal antiquing process. Instead of using a lighter base coat and darker antiquing stain, use a darker base coat and lighter metal or jewel color:

1. Seal plaster and apply a dark base-coat color. The base coat may be a spray-on enamel, an acrylic paint with two coats of protective finish, or a metal or jewel wax thinned with turpentine. You'll never go wrong with an ebony black or rich chocolate brown base coat.

2. After the base coat has dried, apply the metal or jewel color thinly and evenly with your little finger or soft cloth. Be extra careful to use a light touch and a small amount of wax so that the highlight will cover only protruding areas. The dark base-coat color should show through cracks and crevices in the design.

3. When dry, buff if desired, and apply at least two coats of a protective finish. A matte or bisque finish is most compatible with the antique look, although a low or normal gloss allows the highlight to show more sparkle.

Reverse antiquing with highlight colors is beautiful as well as versatile. Like the normal antiquing process, this technique also allows creativity in combining base-coat colors with various highlight colors. Here are a few suggestions to get you started:

Antiquing in Reverse Guide

EFFECT DESIRED	BASE COAT TO USE	HIGHLIGHT TO USE
antique gold	Spanish copper or dark brown	gold
brass	patina or blue-green	gold or brass
bronze	patina or blue-green	copper
Chinese gold	red or orange	gold
gold leaf	black	gold or gold leaf
midnight blue	black	pearl blue or sapphire
pewter	black	silver or pewter
silver leaf	black	silver
Spanish copper	black or brown	copper
Wedgwood	white	pearl blue

Metal and jewel waxes enable you to achieve rich antique effects. The silver dollar, for example, was given a black base coat and highlighted with a silver wax. Painted by Ila Mae Robinson.

Oriental gods (see color section) are especially impressive when antiqued in reverse with a black base coat and gold wax. Courtesy Plast-a-Craft, Inc., Portland, Ore.

"FOILING" PLASTERCRAFT

Another popular way to decorate plastercraft is to cover it with art foil or gold leaf. Both materials give plaster the most realistic metal look possible.

Art foil is by far the easiest to use. Available at hobby stores, art foil is very durable and comes in a variety of colors. (Or use aluminum kitchen foil.) Cut the foil into a piece that will completely cover the plastercraft, including edges. Apply white glue to the plaster and lay the foil in place. Gently tamp the foil with a rag or cotton swab to work it into cracks and crevices. After the glue dries, you may antique the foil or highlight with rub-on waxes if desired.

Gold leafing is more complicated. First seal the plaster and apply a base coat. Red is suggested because the base coat will often glow through the gold leaf. When the base coat is dry, paint the entire piece with a brush-on varnish (or adhesive). When the varnish becomes tacky, lay the small sheets of gold leaf on the varnish, one by one, until the object is completely covered. Pat the gold leaf gently with a cotton ball to make sure it adheres to the varnish. When dry, gently brush or blow off excess gold leafing and spray on a protective finish.

Art foil and gold leafing are both excellent ways to decorate religious designs, ornate frames, fruit compotes, butterflies, and candleholders.

The butterfly is covered with blue art foil and highlighted with silver wax—another popular way to decorate plaster.

CREATING A VELVET TOUCH

A unique way to decorate plaster is to add a velvet touch—for plaster can look and *feel* exactly like rich velvet. You can velvetize plaster either by hand or by machine.

The hand method uses white craft glue and velvet flocking that comes in small bags of various colors at the hobby store. Place the plaster on newspaper or in a box, seal, and cover with glue. Then sprinkle the flocking over the glue by hand or from an old plastic bottle (such as liquid detergent or shampoo comes in). Apply flocking generously and make sure the entire object is covered. When dry, shake off excess flocking.

The machine method is also easy and much more accurate because an electrostatic wand places velvet fibers exactly where you want them. One popular brand is called VelveTouch and is available at hobby stores. Often hobby shops have a machine that you can use for a small charge.

When using the wand, you first apply adhesive on the area you want to be velvetized. Select the color of velvet fiber you desire and guide the wand over the area as you would a crayon. The wand transmits the fibers to the plaster.

This velvet touch is perfect for small dogs and cats, turtles and frogs, small statuary, fruits, and novelty designs. Or, you can velvetize certain areas of the plaster only, such as flowers, pool tables, clothing, etc.

Velvet fibers may be applied by hand or machine to give plaster both the look and feel of thick velvet. Courtesy Plast-a-Craft, Inc., Portland, Ore.

You can add a velvet touch to small areas only, such as the leaves and eyelids of the frog. Courtesy Plast-a-Craft, Inc., Portland, Ore.

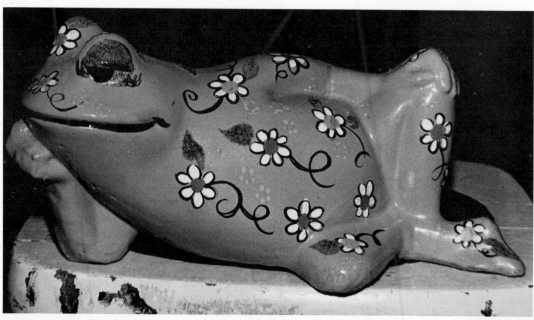

Zodiac plaque. Painted by B. Kay Fraser.

Pool player plaque. Painted by B. Kay Fraser.

Musical owl trio. Courtesy Plast-a-Craft, Inc., Portland, Ore.

"Bugsville" mushroom plaque. Painted by Ila Mae Robinson.

Early American spoon and fork. Painted by B. Kay Fraser.

Young lad in 3-cornered hat. Courte Off the Wall of Eugene, Ore.

Spanish galleon. Courtesy Plast-a-Craft, Inc., Portland, Ore.

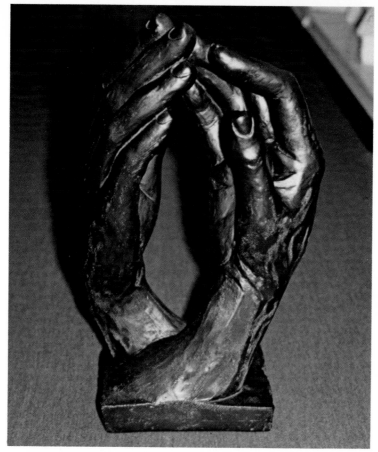

Rodin's "Cathedral." Courtesy Off the Wall of Eugene, Ore.

Hotei figurine. Courtesy Plast-a-Craft, Inc., Portland, Ore.

W. C. Fields figurine. Courtesy Off the Wall of Eugene, Ore.

Sea captain with pipe lampbase. Painted by Laurie Sturrock.

Fruit compote. Courtesy Off the Wall of Eugene, Ore.

Chrysanthemum and rose plaques. Painted by B. Kay Fraser.

Love and Peace signs.
Painted by Tina and Mary Robinson.

Raggedy Ann "paper doll" set. Painted by B. Kay Fraser.

Plaster figurine on tole painted plaque. Painted by Silvia Sauter.

Plaster cast in sand with agates and candle. Created by B. Kay Fraser.

*Armored soldier on horseback.
Courtesy Off the Wall of Eugene, Ore.*

Musical cherubs in matching frames. Painted by B. Kay Fraser.

COMBINING SPECIAL TECHNIQUES

Although the special techniques for plastercraft just described are strong testimony to this craft's versatility, there's still more. Each of the techniques learned so far may be combined to create further methods of self-expression through plastercraft.

For example, you can combine metal waxes with a pearl finish: combine jewel waxes with "wood look" antiquing; combine pearl paints with acrylic colors; combine "metal look" antiquing with brighter metal waxes; combine enamel base coats with velvet flocking and metal waxes.

Successful combinations of techniques are illustrated. The doves, for instance, were given an antique white acrylic base coat; eyes and beak were highlighted with a rub-on gold wax; then the entire bird was sprayed with a pearl finish.

The Winchester plaque combines acrylic paints with "wood look" antiquing and metal waxes. Acrylic base-coat colors are woodtone on the plaque; chocolate brown on the gunstock and forearm; black on the action, barrel, and name plate. After a protective coating to seal the antiquing, the rifle's action and barrel and the lettering on the name plate were highlighted with silver wax. The entire plaque was then protected with a matte finish.

The Spanish galleon (see color section) combines "wood look" antiquing with a multicolored base coat, glass staining dyes, metal waxes, and even hobby optical lights. Base-coat colors are woodtone on background and ship; antique white on sails; red on flags and crosses; and antique gold on waves. A root beer spray dye was then added over the ship, and green and blue glass staining dyes were sprayed over the waves to create an aquamarine color. The entire piece was then antiqued with a fruitwood stain. Rub-on highlights of gold and silver were added where appropriate. After using a final protective finish, tiny hobby optical lights were inserted in windows of the galleon.

Delicate iridescent doves are created by combining an acrylic base coat with a gold wax and pearl finish. Painted by B. Kay Fraser.

This Winchester plaque was made with acrylic base coat colors, "wood look" antiquing, and silver wax. Painted by Duke McCurdy.

An impressive Spanish galleon resulted when four different techniques were combined. Painted by Phillip South, President, Plast-a-Craft, Inc.

6

Perk Up
Plaster Plaques

After seeing plaster plaques with three-dimensional designs, plain plaster plaques without designs may look "ho-hum." But, if you use plaster plaques in the same manner as you use wooden plaques, then the only yawning will be from staying up late to decorate them.

Flat plaster plaques, like wooden plaques, are intended to be used for découpage, tole painting, ecology displays, and so forth. But plaster has the advantage of being cheaper and quicker to work with. For example, the same size wooden plaque that costs at least two dollars can cost thirty-five cents when cast in plaster. A wooden plaque that takes days of drying time can be replaced by a plaster plaque that can be decorated in an hour.

So here are a few ideas to help you perk up plaster plaques.

DÉCOUPAGE TECHNIQUES

Even if you have never experimented with découpage art before, plastercraft can turn you into a découpage artist overnight. The trick is to paint a plaque to simulate wood; add an attractive paper picture; then antique the entire object for shading and depth.

1. Seal plaster plaque, then spray or brush on a base coat. Suggested base-coat colors are woodtone, avocado, red, orange, and harvest yellow. If the print is black and white, the plaque will be especially effective if a bright base-coat color is chosen. If the plaque is intended for a special room, use one of the room colors for a base coat so it will blend well with the decor. If the print is especially bright and colorful, then a woodtone plaque will display it to its best advantage. (If an acrylic base coat is used, seal with a protective finish before proceeding to next step.)

2. Next, select a picture suitable for découpage. Craft stores and catalogs have a nice selection of prints. Greeting cards work well. Or use wedding and anniversary invitations and birth announcements for a découpage souvenir. Avoid thin paper such as magazine pages or wrapping paper because it may wrinkle or tear.

Trim the print to fit the plaque. You may tear the edges; cut with scissors or pinking shears; or burn the edges over a match or candle flame—burn a little at a time, blowing or pinching the flame out when the desired portion has burned.

3. Affix the print to the plaque with white glue or a découpage formula, such as Mod Podge. Use a rag, squeegee, or roller to flatten the print against the plaque and push out air bubbles. The print must be absolutely flat or you'll have unwanted bulges.

4. When the glue has dried—usually ten to twenty minutes—apply two coats of Mod Podge or spray protective finish, allowing drying time between coats.

5. If desired, you may antique the entire plaque and print using methods explained in chapter 4. Walnut, fruitwood, or any brown-colored stain will resemble wood. Allow stain to settle in cracks and crevices around the edge. Remove more stain from the main portion of the print so it is easily visible. Leave more stain around the edge of the print so that it will blend with the plaque. You may wipe the glaze with cheesecloth, a soft lintless rag, old nylon, foam rubber, or paper tissue. Be sure to brush the stain lightly with a soft dry brush, always pulling in the same direction to give the effect of a wood grain.

6. When dry, add at least two coats of protective finish, Mod Podge, or clear varnish. The more coats you add, the richer and more hand waxed the plaque will look.

Plaster plaques may be used for any type of découpage, including transfer art. You may also purchase products that "crackle" and "fracture" the print and plaque for added antique charm.

Assemble plaque, print, and découpage formula.

Tear, cut, or burn the edges of the print and glue to plaster. Presto! instant découpage.

Transfer art découpage is especially effective on oval plaster plaques. Courtesy Plast-a-Craft, Inc., Portland, Ore.

TOLE OR PATTERN PAINTING IDEAS

Another clever way to perk up plain plaster plaques is to borrow a few techniques from tole or pattern painting. Basically, you paint the plaque to resemble wood, trace a pattern on the plaque, then color in the pattern with acrylic or oil paints. Thus, in a few hours, a plain plaster plaque is transformed into a colorful work of art.

1. Paint the plaque to simulate wood, using a woodtone or colored base coat. Antique the plaque as explained in chapter 4, then give it a protective coating. (Or, you may wait to antique until after you have painted the pattern.)

2. Select a pattern to trace onto the plaque. Patterns may be found in tole painting books (see *Decorative Tole Painting* by B. Kay Fraser) or you may copy patterns from greeting cards, magazines, other paintings, needle-point and crewel patterns, or—be completely original—create your own design.

To transfer the pattern to the plaque, first lay the pattern over the plaque so the design is exactly where you want it. Keep the pattern in place by securing with masking tape. Then slip a piece of graphite paper or art transfer paper (sticky side down) between the plaque and pattern. When you trace over the pattern with a soft-leaded pencil, the design is thus transferred to your plaque.

3. Now fill in the design in favorite colors, just as you would the areas of a coloring book. You may use acrylic craft paints, although several coats may be required to cover dark-colored plaques. Or first fill in pattern with white, then use color paints.

Tole artists usually prefer to use artists' oils that have been thinned with varnish for a smoother application. Artists' oils are more easily blended for highlight and shading than acrylic paints.

4. When the paint has dried, give the plaque several coats of protective finish. If you have not antiqued the plaque earlier, do it now. Because the design will also be antiqued, you may need to remove stain in tiny areas with a Q-tip. Seal antiquing with a protective finish. As with découpage, additional coats of finish add additional luster.

Plaster plaques, whether flat or three-dimensional, lend themselves to tole-painting techniques. For example, you can paint a small plaster figurine, then glue it to a plaster or wooden plaque that has a tole-painted background. You can tole-paint any three-dimensional plaque using the plaque's design as a guide instead of a pattern. In fact, the shading, highlights, and color blend-

Trace any pattern onto a plaque with pencil and graphite or art transfer paper.

ing that are possible with artists' oils are superior to those of acrylic craft paints, but not as easy for the beginner.

Still another idea is to combine tole painting and découpage in a memory plaque. Give the plaque a base coat, découpage the wedding or birth announcement, add a tole or pattern design, antique in a wood color, and finish with a protective coating.

A plaster plaque provides an inexpensive background for tole painting.

Combine techniques from plastercraft, découpage, and tole to make a delightful memory plaque.

Tole painting techniques may easily be combined with plastercraft. Use artists' oils thinned with varnish to paint a wooden plaque and plaster figurine.

Use white or craft glue to bond a plaster to wood. The result is a clever combination of tole and plastercraft (see color section). Painted by Silvia Sauter.

ECOLOGY DISPLAYS

A meaningful idea for perking up plain plaques is to show your appreciation of nature—make an ecology display. To do this, glue objects from nature onto a plaster plaque that has been painted and antiqued (optional). Or, use a plaster frame and plastic dome to preserve a natural object.

For example, ecology "bouquets" are made in three easy steps:

1. Prepare plaque by sealing, applying a base coat, antiquing, and spraying ⦁a protective finish. Suggested base-coat colors are woodtone, harvest yellow, orange, red, lime green. Because the bouquet will be in natural colors, a bright background provides pleasing contrast.

2. Select and arrange the bouquet. Strawflowers, stalks of grain, dried grass, and twigs from the backyard are appropriate suggestions. The beauty

of an ecology bouquet is in its simplicity, however, so don't overdo it. In fact, a set of plaques with one natural item to a plaque can be very effective.

3. When the bouquet is arranged to your satisfaction, glue the items in place using a small dab of glue on stems only. Let dry overnight. Or, secure stems in place with a taut band of leather, felt, ribbon, or such. Cut the band to fit and keep it tightly in place by nailing with furniture tacks. Work the tacks into the plaster gently with your thumb or by tapping lightly with a hammer. Too much force will shatter the plaster.

Another clever idea for an ecology plaque comes courtesy of your kitchen cupboard. Arrange dried foods such as beans, peas, dried corn, and macaroni into a picture. A simple technique is:

1. Prepare plaque by sealing and adding a base coat. Bright colors without antiquing are especially gay. Spray-on oil-base colors will not require a protective finish; but acrylic paints should have a finish so glue will not be absorbed.

2. Sketch or trace a design on the plaque. Simple designs of birds, animals, faces, boats, etc., are easiest. Then play with the foods to see which type of bean or pea best fits the design. For example, green peas may be used for leaves and grass, navy beans create interesting trees and limbs, yellow corn kernels can make a sun or mushroom, and red kidney beans are good for facial features. Try to use varied colors and textures.

3. When satisfied with your food selection, glue in place with white glue. Apply glue to a small area at a time and place seeds and beans in glue, using tweezers or fingers. Let dry overnight. A protective finish will aid in preserving food items.

Ecology bouquets require few materials.

Your concern for our environment displays itself in an ecology bouquet.

Ingredients for an ecology food plaque may be found in your kitchen cupboard.

Simple designs are easily created by children, yet are appealing enough to display forever.

PAINTING PLASTER FRAMES

With a little imagination, frames made of plaster can be stunning. For example, you can select a plaster frame to enhance other plaster designs. Decorate the frame to match the design. In the example pictured, both frames and cherubs were given a white base coat, highlighted with a gold wax, then sprayed with a pearl finish. The background is a piece of royal blue velvet glued to a piece of cardboard.

Many frames have hangers that bend to hold the cardboard or picture in place. If they don't, use masking tape and/or glue to affix the cardboard to the frame. If a small design is used, you can glue it to the background. If a larger and therefore heavier plaster design is used, hang the design on a nail punched through the cardboard.

Frames may also be used to show off ecology displays, as described earlier. Glue your bouquet or dried foods to painted or cloth-covered cardboard and insert in the plaster frame. You may also wish to use a plastic dome to protect your natural treasures from the ravages of time.

When plaster frames are used in place of a wood or metal frame, remember that you can decorate the frame to look exactly like wood or metal (chapter 4). Or enhance the picture by using blending or contrasting base-coat colors. For example, if you are framing a black-and-white photograph or picture, use a bright color for contrast. If you are framing a colored photo-

Plaster frames can be decorated to match plaster designs, such as these adorable cherubs (see color section). Painted by B. Kay Fraser.

graph, use a base-coat color that blends with a color in the picture, such as an orange frame to match orange flowers. Antiquing is recommended for colored base coats.

And don't overlook the many special techniques you can use on plaster frames (chapter 5.) Gold leafing is elegant on frames with ornate designs. Velvetized frames are ideal with children's pictures. And friends will appreciate anniversary and wedding invitations framed in plaster decorated to match the occasion, such as golden or silver.

Ornate frames are especially effective when highlighted with a rub-on gold wax. Courtesy Custom Arts, Eugene, Ore.

Select a base-coat color for the frame that either blends or contrasts with the picture. Antiquing and/or highlighting adds depth and richness. Courtesy Custom Arts, Eugene, Ore.

NEVER PARDON YOUR BACK

Often plaster plaques and frames look like works of art from the front, but the backs are horrid. During the painting and antiquing process, colors drip onto the back—the plaster may be bubbled—the hanger may have rusted. The answer is to cover it up.

The easiest way to cover the back is by spraying on a dark-colored paint. That's better than nothing. But an even better way is to cover the back with contact paper, wallpaper, felt, burlap, etc.

1. Set the plaque or frame on the backing material. Use a pencil or felt-tip pen to draw around the edges. Also mark where the hanger is located. Cut to fit, adding a slit for the hanger to come through.

2. Place the backing on the plaster. If not a perfect fit, trim with scissors until it is perfect. Then affix with white glue.

Plaster statuary should also have a backing, preferably of felt or velvet flocking. A backing is not only pretty but practical. Felt prevents plaster from scratching tabletops and walls, and fabric or paper backings prevent plaques from leaving paint or rust marks on the wall.

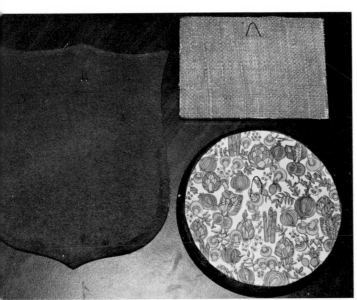

Cover the reverse side of your plaque with fabric or paper.

7

Painting Popular Plaster Designs

Although the many, many ways to decorate plaster make it the ideal hobby for self-expression, sometimes we don't know what to express. To help you select paints and techniques, this final chapter is full of decorating ideas for over seventy of the most popular plaster whiteware designs.

Color suggestions are given here for each piece. For the basic techniques indicated refer to the earlier chapters.

REPRODUCTIONS OF GREAT ART

Perhaps the most exciting plaster designs are those that duplicate the world's great art. Imagine, with plastercraft you can reproduce valuable museum pieces, the hand sculpting of oriental and native craftsmen, and the treasured designs of ancient Greeks and Romans.

Michelangelo's "Pietà" is an excellent example of how easily famous sculptures can be reproduced. To achieve the look of aged marble, 1) apply antique white base coat; 2) antique with black or universal stain; and 3) protect with matte finish. Although the original "Pietà" is housed in the Vatican in Rome, you can now enjoy this sculpture every day in your own home.

Michelangelo's "Pietà." Courtesy Off the Wall of Eugene, Ore.

Young lad in three-cornered hat. Courtesy Off the Wall of Eugene, Ore.

Grecian musician plaques. Courtesy Custom Arts, Eugene, Ore.

The young lad in three-cornered hat (see color section) is a reminder of French Provincial art, popular since the days of Louis XIII. When painting similar busts, apply various colors of acrylic craft paint using light colors first, such as flesh for the body, beige for the pedestal, etc. Continue to medium colors such as blue for the jacket; and finally the darkest color, black, on the hat. You may add highlights to the cheeks, lips, and neck, if desired, with pink chalks or women's makeup. Antique with a raw umber or walnut stain. Protect with a matte finish.

The Grecian musician plaques copy the bas-reliefs of early Greek art and are painted to resemble both antique marble and weathered bronze. The background and flesh are given an antique white (or creme) base coat; all other designs are painted turquoise (moss green will also work). The entire piece is then antiqued with an antique white stain. When dry, accent musical instruments and clothing with copper wax. Seal with a matte finish.

Roman chariot—or Taxicab 36 B.C. Courtesy Plast-a-Craft, Inc., Portland, Ore.

The Roman chariot (or "Taxicab 36 B.C.") is another example of ancient art that can be decorated in an unusual way. This piece has no base coat (although white or antique white could be used). It was merely sealed with a spray lacquer, then antiqued with a moss green stain. After protecting the antique stain with a spray finish, the design was highlighted with a yellow spray dye (or glass-staining paint). The result is a Roman fresco.

The Ming vase proves that ancient Asian craftsmen were just as active and creative as the Europeans. This vase is impressively reproduced by using a base-coat color highlighted with rub-on jewel waxes. The Ming vase shown, for example, was given an Empire blue base coat then antiqued in a Van Dyke stain (a brownish-black color). After sealing the stain, the relief designs were accented with amethyst wax. A matte finish completed the effect of ageless elegance.

Ming vase. Courtesy Off the Wall of Eugene, Ore.

Chinese dragon. Courtesy Off the Wall of Eugene, Ore.

A Chinese dragon is further testimony to the skill of Far Eastern crafts-men. You can display your skill, too, by decorating the dragon in vivid metal and jewel colors. The dragon shown requires 1) a gold base coat, 2) high gloss finish, 3) universal antiquing stain, 4) another coat of high-gloss finish, 5) rub-on jewel waxes of jade for scales and ruby for tongue, 6) a final protective coating of low gloss or matte finish.

The oriental dancers in headdresses completes our selection of great oriental art. These pieces were given a bright orange base coat, then antiqued with walnut stain and highlighted with gold wax. Protective coats of high gloss finish were given after antiquing and after waxing.

Not to be outdone by European and Asian artists, natives of South and Central America and Africa have also produced intriguing masterpieces.

Oriental dancers in headdresses. Courtesy Custom Arts, Eugene, Ore.

The Inca owl, for instance, is treasured for its simplicity and grace. This owl is stunning when "reverse antiqued" with a black base coat highlighted with copper wax. The antique copper effect is enhanced by a matte finish.

Aztec calendars not only demonstrate the high degree of intelligence in that culture but enable us to decorate our homes with museum pieces. Aztec calendars are most effectively decorated with "metal look" antiquing or with bright vivid colors so loved by the Aztecs. If you prefer the metal look, use a gold, silver, or copper base coat and antique with universal (black) stain. (Or, use moss green stain if you want the metal to appear oxidized.)

If you prefer vivid colors, apply acrylic craft paints in orange, red, purple, yellow, fuchsia, hot pink, etc. For the ultimate in brightness, protect with a high gloss finish and do not antique.

Aztec calendar with "metal look." Painted by Marcella Hooey.

This Aztec calendar duplicates the original which is housed at the Museum of Anthropology in Mexico City. Painted by B. Kay Fraser.

The black mother and child is a wonderful reminder of the beauty of African people. This graceful piece of statuary resembles ivory black when you 1) use a black base coat, 2) antique with pearl luster or antique white stain, and 3) seal with a matte finish. Or, you may use a black base coat and spray with a pearl finish.

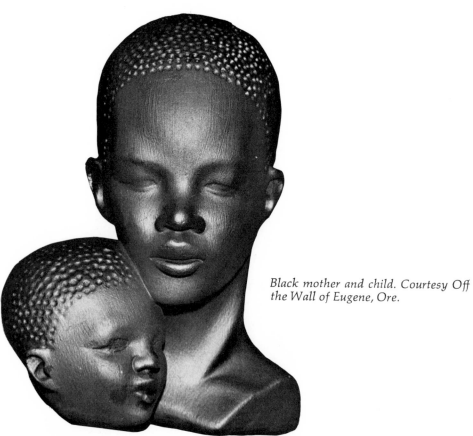

Black mother and child. Courtesy Off the Wall of Eugene, Ore.

Spanish shield. Courtesy Custom Arts, Eugene, Ore.

Spanish conquistador in armor. Courtesy Custom Arts, Eugene, Ore.

Spanish conquistador on wooden background. Courtesy Plast-a-Craft, Inc., Portland, Ore.

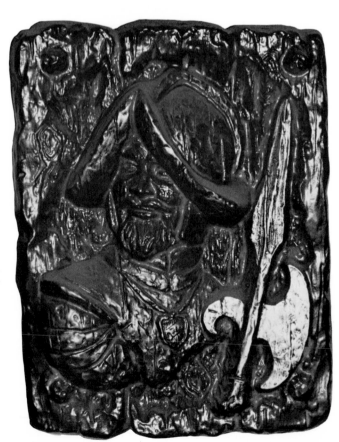

THE MEDITERRANEAN MOTIF

Mediterranean, or early Spanish, designs are extremely popular among plastercraft artists, probably because many homes boast this elegant motif. As you know, the Spanish favored rich browns and blacks highlighted by shiny gold, copper, and silver. For this reason, most Mediterranean designs should feature "metal look" antiquing or reverse antiquing with metal waxes.

The Spanish shield, for example, was transformed into a Mediterranean treasure by "metal look" antiquing. The entire piece was sprayed with a gold base coat, then black was sprayed around the edges only. Next, the plaque was antiqued with a universal (black) stain. The stain was allowed to settle darkly in low areas, but nearly all stain was removed from relief areas so that the gold would glimmer richly through. A low gloss finish enables the gold to shine a bit without ruining the antique look.

Spanish conquistadores are also popular designs. When painting conquistadores in armor, apply a spray-on silver base coat and antique with universal stain. A low-gloss finish is complementary to armor.

When painting conquistadores on "wooden" plaques, a bit more color is suggested. On the plaque shown, the entire piece was given a nutmeg base coat, then antiqued with a fruitwood stain. After protecting with a gloss finish, rub-on waxes were used for color highlights: gold on helmet and medal, silver on blade, and ruby on garment. A low gloss or matte finish should complete this impressive wall hanging.

A Spanish sword achieves a realistic effect through reverse antiquing. After applying a black base coat, add color with rub-on waxes. Use silver for the blade, emerald for leaves, gold for handle, and ruby for decorative accents. Finish with a matte or low gloss.

A Mediterranean candleholder is a welcome accent to any room with Spanish decor. Apply a metal-colored base coat such as gold, copper, or silver; then antique with a universal stain. Although the candleholder is extremely easy to make, it will look exactly like old Spanish metal.

Spanish sword. Courtesy Plast-a-Craft, Inc., Portland, Ore.

Mediterranean candleholder. Courtesy Plast-a-Craft, Inc., Portland, Ore.

Spanish dancing girl. Courtesy Plast-a-Craft, Inc., Portland, Ore.

The Spanish dancing girl is a joy to look at and a joy to paint—if you like projects that challenge your creativity. One artist created this stunning interpretation with rub-on jewel and metal waxes. Here's how: 1) Spray the entire piece with a black base coat. 2) Apply rub-on waxes using onyxite (coppery black) for skin; sapphire for blouse and fan; gold for earrings, shoes, and skirt highlights; ruby or rose for lips, roses, and flowers in skirt; and emerald for headdress trim and leaves in skirt. 3) Protect with a normal gloss finish.

A Mediterranean ashtray duplicates the look of heavy Spanish wood and metal brads. To achieve this effect, use a woodtone base coat and paint the brads black. Antique with walnut stain. Add shine to the brads with pewter wax. Protect with matte finish.

Mediterranean ashtray. Courtesy Off the Wall of Eugene, Ore.

A Mediterranean lamp base and other styles enable you to have decorator lamps in your home for less than half than you would pay at a store. The Mediterranean lamp base shown *(far right)* is created by painting the metal parts black and the wooden part a woodtone color. Seal with matte finish, then antique with a Van Dyke or walnut stain, and seal again.

The more contemporary lamp base in the middle was given a black base coat and highlighted with silver wax. The lamp base on the left is very colorful with a yellow base coat, patina (or moss green) antiquing stain, and turquoise wax highlights added to the bumpy areas. A high gloss finish was used after base-coating, antiquing, and when completed.

Lamp bases made of plaster. Courtesy Off the Wall of Eugene, Ore.

EARLY AMERICAN DESIGNS

Favorite relics from America's past are a welcome addition to any home that features the warm, comfortable look of Early American. Best yet, by painting plaster designs, you can reproduce "antiques" that would cost a great deal in an antique shop.

The secret of making plaster antiques appear authentic is a technique you already know—"wood look" antiquing. Wood color stains of walnut, fruitwood, etc., transform painted plaster into a mellow, aged antique. A matte or bisque finish adds the perfect finishing touch.

The Royal Tavern inn sign, for example, is a replica of a typical sign used in early days. Yet it looks like the original painted wood sign rather than a plaster replica because the artist made excellent use of antiquing stain. Here's how to duplicate this inn sign: 1) apply a base coat of red on the wooden background and black on the lion and lettering; 2) seal with matte finish; 3) antique with a wood-color stain; 4) seal with matte finish; 5) rub a gold wax on lion and lettering; and 6) seal again with matte finish.

Royal Tavern inn sign. Courtesy Off the Wall of Eugene, Ore.

The Continental soldier, federal eagle on badge, and military drum also duplicate the look of authentic painted wood. A raw umber (or walnut) antiquing stain and matte finish did the trick. Base-coat colors for the soldier are white stockings, cravat, and gunpowder horn; flesh hands and neck; gray vest and cuffs; blond hair; royal blue jacket; brown pants, rifle, thong, and log; black shoes, hat, and eyes. After antiquing, a silver wax may be added to shoe buckles and buttons.

The federal eagle is base-coated in white, tan, and brown with mustard yellow beak and talons. The shield is appropriately colored red, white, and blue with mustard-yellow stars and dark green leaves.

The military drum is base-coated in cheerful colors of red, white, and blue with a brown eagle and mustard-yellow braid and buttons.

Continental soldier, federal eagle on badge, and military drum plaques. Courtesy Off the Wall of Eugene, Ore.

Federal eagle with wings spread. Courtesy Custom Arts, Eugene, Ore.

The *federal eagle* may also be painted with "metal look" antiquing techniques to create an authentic-looking replica. Spray on a gold, silver, or copper base coat, then antique with a universal stain. Complete with a matte finish.

The *buffalo nickel and Indian head penny* are further examples of how to reproduce collectors' items with "metal look" antiquing. The nickels were base-coated with spray-on silver and antiqued with universal stain. The pennies were base-coated with spray-on copper and antiqued with universal stain (a moss green stain may be used for an oxidized copper effect). If desired, coins may instead be "reverse antiqued" by base-coating with spray-on black, then highlighted with silver or copper wax. As usual, a matte or bisque finish is recommended.

Buffalo nickel and Indian head penny. Painted by Ila Mae Robinson.

Early American clock. Courtesy Custom Arts, Eugene, Ore.

An Early American clock is a clever way to combine beauty with practicality. The plaster design was given a medium brown base coat, then antiqued with a walnut stain. After sealing with a matte finish, the clockworks were inserted. Clockworks are available at hobby shops or where plaster whiteware is sold.

Antique dueling pistols are a welcome addition to the den or trophy room. Few people will believe the wood and metal designs are actually painted plaster. To make your pistol plaque look as real as the one shown: 1) apply base-coat colors of woodtone for the frame and background (background may also be blue, red, or green) and brown for the entire pistol; 2) seal and antique with Van Dyke or walnut; 3) seal and apply gold wax to handle accents and trigger, and silver wax to action and barrels. Protect with matte finish.

Dueling pistol plaque. Courtesy Off the Wall of Eugene, Ore.

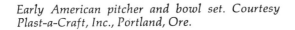

Early American pitcher and bowl set. Courtesy Plast-a-Craft, Inc., Portland, Ore.

An Early American pitcher and bowl set is a lovely way to bring this decor into bedrooms and even bathrooms. Original pitcher and bowl sets were usually made of white ironstone or painted china. So decorate sets as plain or fancy as you wish—the pioneers did.

On the pitcher and bowl set illustrated, the pieces were given a nutmeg (light brown) base coat and antiqued with a fruitwood stain. After sealing, add color with jewel waxes—sapphire for flowers, emerald for leaves and borders. A normal gloss finish was the final touch.

If you prefer a white ironstone or bone china background, use a white base coat and antique white stain.

Early American grinder plaques bring antique beauty into the kitchen. Let the plaster design be your guide: use a light woodtone on the background; green on ivy and stems; medium brown or black on grinder boxes; and black on metal handles, wheels, and trim. Seal and antique with walnut or fruitwood. Use gold wax to highlight metal trim and wheels. Or use silver wax on the coffee grinder *(left)* and gold wax on the pepper grinder *(right)*.

An alternate idea for grinder plaques is to use an antique white background and paint the grinders red or woodtone.

Coffee and pepper grinder plaques. Painted by Ila Mae Robinson.

73

Early American keys. Painted by Marcella Hooey.

Early American keys complete the selection of popular designs in an antique motif. Because original keys were made of metal, it is recommended that you always decorate key plaques with metal colors. On the keys shown, the artist used the reverse antiquing method to achieve an aged brass effect. The keys were given a black base coat, then liberally covered with an olive-bronze wax. The relief designs were highlighted with gold wax. Finally, the keys were protected with a matte finish.

LIVING THINGS—PEOPLE, BIRDS, ANIMALS

Painting plaques and statuary of people, birds, and animals is as much fun and as popular as painting any of the other designs shown so far. But it can be more of a challenge. Color selection is more critical when painting living things because these designs should be as realistically colored as possible. You'll find that friends and family are instant critics if you goof on color selection.

Instructions here will guide you through many popular designs. Or thumb through outdoor magazines to find realistic colors for game birds, animals, and fish. Gift stores and catalogs often show ceramic figurines of people that can give you color ideas. Public libraries are an excellent source of books with colored pictures of birds, animals, and fish as well as books with famous paintings and sculpture that you can copy on figurines. When in doubt, find out.

The "character" lamp bases will begin instructions for painting people because both figures have been realistically reproduced through clever use of antiquing stain. Heavy antiquing is the secret to giving faces and hands a weathered appearance. Walnut, fruitwood, or Van Dyke stains are all effective.

"The helmsman" is wearing gray rain gear and black boots and has blond hair. The woodtone ship's wheel is mounted to a black column and brown base with gray anchor designs. (An alternate idea is to paint a brunet helmsman wearing yellow rain gear.)

74

"The helmsman" lamp base. Painted by David Sturrock.

"Sea captain with pipe" lamp base. Painted by Laurie Sturrock.

"The sea captain with pipe" (see color section) is wearing a brown jacket and cap with yellow buttons and trim, antique white pants, and black shoes. He is blond and is carrying a black pipe. A black base completes this lamp design. (Another color scheme could be navy blue jacket and cap, white pants, and red base.)

After sealing, these base-coat colors are blended and mellowed by the antiquing stain, which also shades and accents facial features and wrinkles. Use heavy antiquing on similar character designs, such as cowboys, pirates, soldiers, etc.

The boy and girl bookends, on the other hand, were very lightly antiqued with walnut stain . . . their youthful features would be ruined by heavy antiquing. Yet the stain did add depth and shading to grass, hair, hat, and stumps. Both the boy and girl were base-coated with white shirts; flesh face, hands, and feet, blond hair, and red lips. A bright green base coat was used

Boy and girl bookends. Painted by B. Kay Fraser.

for the grass, and a medium brown one for stump. The girl figurine has a red jumper, scarf and polka-dot blouse, a yellow bird and flowers. The boy figurine has medium blue overalls and polka-dot shirt, light blue bird, and tan straw hat. After antiquing, they were sealed with a matte finish.

Notice the eyes. Quite often plaster whiteware will have indentations for eyes, but no definite shape for eyeball, lashes, and brows. To paint eyes, first paint the whole eye white; then add a colored iris such as blue, green, or brown (when light colors are chosen, you can also add a black pupil); finally outline the eye with dark brown or black using a small round-tipped brush and add eyebrows and/or lashes. Be sure each color is dry before continuing to the next color.

If desired, you may seal the figurine with a spray finish before attempting the eyes. By doing so, you can wipe off mistakes with a rag or tissue until you get the eyes just the way you want them. Seal again before antiquing.

Another hint for painting children is that you can give a youthful blush to the cheeks with pink chalk or women's makeup. You can also substitute women's eye liner for painting lashes and brows.

The African woman and African warrior are examples of different ways to paint black flesh. The woman's flesh was painted dark brown, antiqued in universal stain, and sealed with matte finish. The warrior's flesh was painted a rich copper brown, was not antiqued, and was sealed with a gloss finish. Other base-coat colors on the woman are black hair, red robes, and yellow vessel. The warrior has black hair, purple robe, and tan shield.

African woman and African warrior. Courtesy Off the Wall of Eugene, Ore.

The large bull elephant demonstrates that realism is just as possible with animals as with people. Although the elephant looks like a valuable heirloom, he is very easy to paint. In fact, with the exception of ivory tusks and brown eyes, he is, like most elephants, gray. A walnut antiquing stain adds rich shading to the elephant's hide. Seal with a matte finish and you'll have an intriguing piece of plaster statuary that sells for around sixty dollars in gift shops.

Large bull elephant. Courtesy Off the Wall of Eugene, Ore.

The king of beasts shows another exciting yet simple way to paint large statuary. The lion in the foreground was given a woodtone base coat highlighted with a root beer spray dye around tail, mane, and paws. He was then antiqued with a fruitwood stain to shade facial features, mane, and tail. The lighter-colored lion in the background was given a yellow base coat and antiqued heavily with walnut. Both methods produce a charming, realistic king of beasts.

King of beasts. Courtesy Custom Arts, Eugene, Ore.

Collie and Irish setter plaques bring man's best friend into the home. Looking silky enough to pet, these plaques were painted with artists' oil in appropriate colors. Artists' oils may be used successfully on plaster if the oil is thinned with varnish—otherwise, they tend to streak.

When painting dogs with acrylic craft paints, select colors that match the breed of dog you are painting. Antiquing is recommended using a stain color that most nearly matches the natural shading of the breed: for example, burnt umber (a reddish brown) on Irish setters, walnut on collies, light fruitwood on cocker spaniels, etc. Black Labrador retrievers are very effective when base-coated in black and highlighted with an antique white stain or simply base-coated in black and sealed with a pearl finish.

Collie and Irish setter heads. Courtesy Custom Arts, Eugene, Ore.

Deer plaques can be attractive when painted to resemble a piece of hand-carved wood. Use the "wood look" antiquing method with a woodtone base coat and walnut or fruitwood antiquing stain. Seal with a matte finish.

The long-horn steer gained beauty and realism through a combination of special techniques: 1) apply a woodtone base coat to entire piece; 2) paint tips and ends of horns black, and paint eyes white and black; 3) seal and antique with universal (black); 4) accent head only with root beer spray dye; 5) apply rub-on silver wax to horns; 6) seal with matte finish; 7) glue on false eyelashes.

Deer plaques. Painted by Wick McCurdy.

Longhorn steer. Courtesy Custom Arts, Eugene, Ore.

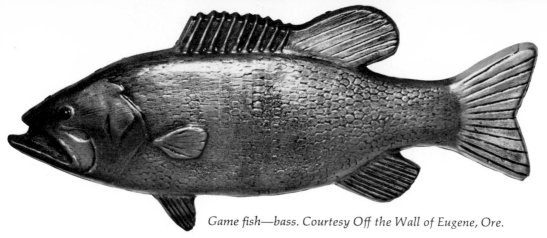

Game fish—bass. Courtesy Off the Wall of Eugene, Ore.

The game fish (a bass) is a prime example of how rub-on waxes can simulate nature's underwater color scheme, too. Best of all, a plaster fish can't break the line, making it an excellent gift for sportsmen who moan about the "one that got away." You can create the bass in three easy steps: 1) apply a silver base coat; 2) antique heavily with universal stain; 3) seal, then delicately rub hints of emerald and sapphire on the body of the fish and silver on tail and fins. Use a high gloss finish between steps and to protect—fish are shiny when they leap out of water.

Owl designs prove that plastercraft is very definitely for the birds, too! Owls can be painted to resemble wood or metal, in bright fun colors to accent a room's decor, or to look like real owls.

"The musical owl trio," for example, was decorated in both bright and wood colors (see color section). A woodtone base coat was sprayed on the entire object. The owls were colored orange with white masks and black

Musical owl trio. Courtesy Plast-a-Craft, Inc., Portland, Ore.

Large-eyed owl. Courtesy Custom Arts, Eugene, Ore.

Pointed-eye owl set. Courtesy Custom Arts, Eugene, Ore.

eyes. Fruitwood antiquing added rich depth and wood graining. Finally, the musical instruments, beaks, and talons were highlighted with gold wax. A high gloss finish was used between steps and as a protective coating.

The imaginative "large-eyed owl" is decorated with glass staining paints. 1) Apply a spray-on gold base coat; 2) add black eye outline, eyes, and talons; 3) Seal and apply glass staining paints (or spray dyes) as explained in chapter 5, creating new colors as you spray.

"The pointed-eye owl set" fits well in an avocado-colored kitchen because of the colors chosen. These owls were given yellow masks, avocado green bodies, orange beaks, talons, and eye liner, and a woodtone branch. The owls were antiqued with a walnut stain and sealed with a normal gloss finish.

Wild partridges are another delightful bird design. The pair shown gained their realistic coloring through an antique white base coat and heavy walnut antiquing. A matte finish was selected. Another stunning—though not as realistic—way to paint this design is to use a dark brown base coat and highlight with rub-on copper wax.

Wild partridges. Painted by B. Kay Fraser.

The fighting cock is a very popular design both in statuary and plaques. A beautifully colored rooster is easy to create with five acrylic craft paints and walnut antiquing stain. For the base coat, use yellow on the pear, beak, and legs; red on entire head and tail, caramel on the lower half of body, brown on upper half and base of statue, green on leaves. Seal and wipe with walnut stain. Protect with a matte finish.

The pheasants in spring plaque is an extremely beautiful design and should be painted with tender loving care. When using acrylic craft paints, remember that pheasant chicks are born in the spring and therefore appropriate spring colors should be used.

On the plaque shown, the artist selected a combination of special techniques rather than using acrylic craft paints. You can duplicate the effect: 1) apply a woodtone base coat over the entire plaque; 2) apply suitable color to leaves, flowers, cattails, and trees by using artists' oils thinned with varnish

—pitty-pat the color onto the plaque with tiny pieces of foam rubber; 3) seal, then antique heavily with one part burnt umber artists' oil mixed with one part paint thinner (homemade antiquing stain was selected because it can be worked over a longer period of time without drying); seal and apply color to birds with rub-on waxes using copper for the hen and gold for the chicks. The rooster was colored with rub-on emerald for the head, copper for under-body and tail, gold for beak and talons, combined silver, emerald, and sapphire for outer feathers. Both hen and rooster have white eyes outlined in red, and the rooster has a white ring around his neck. Cattails, flowers, and leaves were also highlighted with rub-on waxes. A matte finish completed this extraordinary design.

Fighting cock statue. Courtesy Off the Wall of Eugene, Ore.

Pheasants in spring plaque. Painted by B. Kay Fraser.

Bugsville mushroom plaque. Painted by Ila Mae Robinson.

FUN WITH FRUIT AND FLOWERS

Fruit and flower designs may be painted realistically enough to fool Mother Nature. Just use the great outdoors as a guide to color schemes.

Mushroom designs are by far the most popular in this category—in fact, mushroom and owl plaques are the most popular of all plastercraft designs.

"The Bugsville mushroom plaque" (see color section) is very large and therefore provides many enjoyable hours of painting fun. On the plaque shown, the artist selected realistic bug and mushroom colors enhanced by a light tan background and "wood look" frame. Mushroom caps are painted in brown, cream, yellow, avocado, orange, bright red, and pink. A white pearl paint gave a realistic touch to shells and shaggy mane mushrooms. After sealing with a normal gloss finish, the entire plaque was antiqued with a mixture of one part burnt umber artists' oil and one part paint thinner. The frame was antiqued heavily to create a wood look, and the mushroom designs were antiqued lightly, just enough stain remaining to mellow colors and shade crevices in the design. Finally, the plaque was sprayed with a clear varnish finish.

Often mushroom plaques are in pairs, such as the "Mushrooms with frog and snail plaques" shown. When painting pairs, be sure to use the same

Mushroom set with frog and snail. Courtesy Plast-a-Craft, Inc., Portland, Ore.

Pattern painted mushrooms on plaque. Courtesy Plast-a-Craft, Inc., Portland, Ore.

colors on both plaques, although the colors may be used on different parts of the design. The same colors aid in creating a coordinated effect. On the set shown, both plaques were given a nutmeg base coat, then brighter colors were added: yellow on mushroom cap designs, light green on stems and undercaps, avocado green on frog, and white and orange on snail. Black was added to eyes. After sealing with a normal gloss spray, both plaques were antiqued with dark fruitwood stain. Seal again with a gloss finish.

Another fun technique with mushrooms is to make your own. Simply sketch or trace a mushroom design on a plaster plaque as explained in chapter 6. Then paint with acrylic craft paints or use tole painting techniques. Seal with a high gloss finish. On the mushroom plaque shown, the artist added dimension to the mushroom design by undercoating mushrooms with white glue (artist's gel may also be used).

The strawberries on wooden scoop demonstrates how realistic fruit can be when painted with acrylic craft paints and then antiqued for shading. For the base coat, apply a woodtone color on the wooden scoop and stem; medium green on leaves; red on berries; and tiny yellow dots on strawberry seeds. After sealing with a gloss finish, wipe with a walnut stain and seal again.

Strawberries on wooden scoop. Courtesy Custom Arts, Eugene, Ore.

The vegetable bouquet on wooden plaque was also painted with acrylic craft paints and antiqued with walnut stain for shading. Apply woodtone to the background, then paint in appropriate vegetable colors beginning with lighter colors first. A low gloss finish works well before and after antiquing.

Vegetable bouquet on wooden plaque. Courtesy Custom Arts, Eugene, Ore.

Glass-stained fruit swag. Courtesy Custom Arts, Eugene, Ore.

The fruit swag shows that special techniques can be used on fruit, for this plaque was decorated with glass staining spray dyes. As you remember from chapter 5, you can create colors as you spray. First give the plaque a gold base coat, then spray yellow and a touch of green on pears, red with a hint of yellow highlight on apples, red and blue to create purple grapes, yellow with a touch of red to create peaches, emerald with a yellow highlight on leaves, and root beer for stems. Additional depth and shading are added by using the root beer spray dye after the other colors have dried. No protective finish is necessary unless you want to mellow colors with a matte finish or give additional sheen with a high gloss finish.

The grape cluster plaque illustrates another impressive technique for fruit—the use of metal and jewel waxes. The entire plaque was given a woodtone base coat, the leaves were painted green and the grapes purple. The plaque was then antiqued heavily with a fruitwood stain. After sealing, wax highlights were applied—green amber (or emerald) on leaves, amethyst on grapes, and gold on stem. A high gloss finish gives the plaque a sunshine sparkle.

Grape cluster plaque. Courtesy Plast-a-Craft, Inc., Portland, Ore.

The small fruit designs demonstrate still another technique for decorating fruit. This technique is borrowed from tole painting because artists' oil thinned with varnish is used and the colors are blended with a tiny piece of foam rubber rather than a brush. Because this color blending technique is extremely beautiful, you may wish to try it. To paint the orange, for example, brush a ring of burnt sienna around the edge of the fruit, yellow in the center, and orange on the remainder. Blend the shade color (burnt sienna) first by pitty-patting with foam rubber, working your way from the edge to the middle. Then, using a clean piece of foam rubber, blend the highlight color (yellow) from the center to the middle. If paint spreads onto the leaf, remove with a paintbrush dipped in paint thinner or turpentine. When dry, paint leaf and stem in suitable colors. Protect with a low gloss or satin finish.

On the apple, use burnt sienna for shading, red for main color, and yellow for highlight. On the peach, use yellow for main color and both burnt sienna and red for shading the edge and center cheek.

Blend fruits painted with artists' oils by using a piece of foam rubber.

Small fruit designs. Painted by B. Kay Fraser.

Round daisy plaque. Painted by Silvia Sauter.

The round daisy plaque also employs tole painting techniques, although you can easily substitute acrylic craft paints. The flowers and background were painted yellow; the leaves and vase are olive green. After sealing, apply burnt umber antiquing stain. Antique heavily—this gives the plaque rich shading and makes it appear that you have used many shades of yellow and green. Protect with low gloss or satin finish.

The flower tree is a lovely example of how acrylic craft paints give beauty to flowers. The flowers were painted in various shades of yellow, orange, and brown; and the basket is light tan. The artist cleverly mixed these colors to create additional coordinating hues for the flowers. After sealing, the flower tree was antiqued with a walnut stain; dark stain remained between flowers and in crevices while the stain was almost completely removed from flower petals and centers. A matte finish completed this work.

Flower tree figurine. Courtesy Custom Arts, Eugene, Ore.

Trillium and clover blossom plaque. Courtesy Custom Arts, Eugene, Ore.

The large *trillium and clover blossom plaque* is exquisite with a touch of pearl paint. Apply brush-on pearl paint in white, pink, or purple to the trilliums, or use normal acrylic craft paints and spray with a pearl finish. Other plaque colors should be woodtone for the background, bright green for leaves, brown for cattails, and yellow, purple, or white for clover blossoms. Seal with a high gloss finish, then antique with walnut or burnt umber. Remove most of the stain from trilliums so the pearl will show through, and leave more stain on the background for a wood grain effect. Seal with a low gloss or satin finish.

The rose decanter set demonstrates the beauty of metal and jewel waxes on flower designs. The decanters were given a nutmeg (rich medium brown) base coat, then antiqued with universal (black) stain. The stain was mostly removed from the smooth surface, and remained thick and dark in the nubbly center. After sealing with normal gloss, rub-on waxes were applied: ruby on roses, gold on leaves and stems. Another coating of normal gloss completed this charming set.

Rose decanter set. Courtesy Plast-a-Craft, Inc., Portland, Ore.

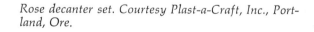

Praying hands plaque. Courtesy Custom Arts, Eugene, Ore.

RELIGIOUS AND CHRISTMAS INSPIRATIONS

Plastercraft religious blessings and inspirations can enhance your wall and your day. Although religious designs can be painted by any method discussed in earlier chapters, it is recommended that you use antiquing stain and mellow or metal colors to create plaques in good taste.

The praying hands plaque, for example, is simple and tasteful when painted to resemble a bronze sculpture. Use a bronze base coat and universal (black) antiquing stain. Protect with a matte finish.

Alternate ideas for this popular religious design are to use a silver or gold base coat antiqued with universal stain; a woodtone base coat antiqued with walnut stain for a wood-grain effect; or a cream or antique white and a walnut stain for a carved ivory look.

The Last Supper is perhaps the most beautiful of religious themes. This plaque can be painted with acrylic craft paints in various colors then antiqued with walnut stain. However, it is often more effective when painted to resemble pounded silver. Apply a silver base coat, then antique with universal stain and seal with matte finish.

Alternate ideas are to use Shadow-Glo paints; to apply a black or dark brown base coat and highlight with gold wax; or to apply an antique white base coat, wipe with walnut stain, and seal with a pearl finish.

Last Supper scene. Courtesy Custom Arts, Eugene, Ore.

Large one-piece Nativity scene. Courtesy Off the Wall of Eugene, Ore.

The Nativity scene is a beautiful one-piece design that can stand by itself on mantels and centerpieces. The artist wisely selected bright colors to paint the figures and a light tan for the wall. When antiqued with burnt umber, the figures are transformed into mellow colors rich with shading and the wall becomes sun-dried adobe brick.

Oak leaf candleholders will be much easier to paint than the Nativity scene, but can also add cheerfulness to Christmas decor. Use woodtone for cones and base and medium green for boughs. Antique heavily with a walnut stain and seal with a gloss finish.

Oak leaf candleholders. Painted by B. Kay Fraser.

Christmas tree decorations. Painted by Lavila, Janet, Tina, and Mary Robinson.

Large Santa Claus. Courtesy Off the Wall of Eugene, Ore.

Christmas ornaments are not only a delightful and inexpensive way to decorate your tree, but can provide hours of enjoyment for the whole family. In fact, painting Christmas ornaments is an excellent project for Scout groups, shut-ins, and for letting children participate in the fun of decorating for Christmas. Use bright-colored acrylic paints and seal with a high gloss finish.

A large Santa Claus completes our selection of religious and Christmas designs. This cuddly Santa was painted with acrylic craft paints in appropriate flesh, white, red, and black colors and sealed with a high gloss finish. No antiquing is needed. For extra color on cheeks and tip of nose, use a bright pink chalk or rouge.

NOVELTY AND YOUTH DESIGNS

You've seen how plastercraft can enhance living room decor, adult bedrooms and kitchens. Novelty and youth designs can also bring plastercraft into dens, party rooms, and children's bedrooms.

Best yet, novelty and youth designs are fun and easy to paint. Antiquing is optional—in fact, most children don't like the darker shading of an antiquing stain. Color selections may be as wild or as sedate as you like. And youth designs often cost under a dollar, making plastercraft an inexpensive hobby for youngsters, too.

There is one word of caution regarding these designs, however. Because little or no antiquing is used, you must be extra-careful to paint accurately. Antiquing stain can hide mistakes, but without it your handiwork is open to inspection. So be sure to follow the Top Ten Tips given in chapter 3 to minimize painting errors.

Horse head chess pieces.
Painted by Marcella Hooey.

The horse head chess pieces are another clever idea for the party room, especially where chess fans match wits. These impressive pieces gained their beauty in four steps: 1) seal and apply a nutmeg color base coat, 2) antique with fruitwood stain, 3) seal with matte finish, and 4) rub on highlights with gold wax and seal again.

German beer steins are also appropriate designs for the party room. If you drink out of the steins, however, you'll find that plaster can drink as much as you. Plaster is very porous and therefore shouldn't be used for drinking purposes. However, you can insert a small vase or baby food jar inside the stein to hold freshly cut flowers or a dry flower arrangement.

The two steins shown are both extremely attractive and were painted with entirely different techniques. The stein on the left received its color through an oriental bamboo base coat antiqued with patina (or moss green) stain. The stein on the right was hand painted with acrylic craft paints, then antiqued with walnut stain. Both steins were sealed with a high gloss finish.

Youth designs, especially those appealing to teen-agers can be appropriate for party rooms as well as teen-age bedrooms. Teen-agers are particularly fond of plaques with lettering.

German beer steins. Courtesy of Off the Wall of Eugene, Ore.

Panic button. Painted by Janet Robinson.

The *Panic Button* not only delights teen-agers but may be appreciated in the office. The panic button has a bright blue background with red and yellow lettering and a flame red button. It was sealed with a high gloss finish.

The *musical kids quartet* adds the charm of bright colors and happy sounds to everyday walls. These figures were painted with vivid colors, then sealed with a high gloss finish. No antiquing needed.

Musical kids quartet. Courtesy Custom Arts, Eugene, Ore.

The *boy and frog in tub* plaque also was not antiqued and leads us into designs for younger children. This adorable plaque was base-coated with acrylic craft paint colors and given added interest by painting the tub with a brush-on white pearl paint. Seal with a high gloss finish.

The Humpty Dumpty design, an example of favorite storybook characters, shows how small plaques can be mounted on wooden or plaster plaques. Glue the plaster plaque to the background plaque, or insert small nail in wooden plaque to hang plaster. The following colors were used on Humpty Dumpty: white on face and brick mortar, yellow and orange on flower, lime green on leaves, medium green on grass, red on bricks and mouth, royal blue on pants and eyes, and brown on branch, hair, and eyebrows. After sealing, the figure was antiqued very lightly with walnut stain. The wooden plaque was also stained with walnut to match. Both Humpty Dumpty and the background plaque were finished with high gloss.

Clown with balloon figurines. Courtesy Custom Arts, Eugene, Ore.

The clown with balloon figurines shows that statuary can be as suitable for the younger set as plaques. In fact, many figurines are hollow-poured so they can be used as penny banks. The clowns pictured were hand painted in bright acrylic colors, then lightly antiqued with fruitwood. A high gloss finish completed the design.

IT'S ONLY THE BEGINNING

We've come to the end of the book—but it's only the beginning of a creative hobby that will last a lifetime. Unlike many hobbies, plastercraft never becomes "old hat." There are so many techniques, so many different paints, and so many clever designs that you can never run out of ideas for decorating plaster.

Plastercraft offers you more than a means of creative self-expression, however. By decorating plaster designs, you can own duplicates of museum masterpieces and collectors' antiques. You can decorate living rooms and kitchens with exquisite plaques that would cost a fortune if purchased in a gift shop. You can add color and interest to family rooms and bedrooms with plaster plaques and statuary.

In addition to adding beauty to your own home with plastercraft, you can create charming gifts for the homes of friends and family. The multitude of designs and colors makes it possible for you to individualize every gift by selecting designs that appeal to your friends and colors that complement their home.

Another bonus of plastercraft is sharing the fun with others. Many friends and family members spend enjoyable afternoons or evenings painting together.

But the greatest reward of plastercraft is the individual thrill you will feel when you transform a piece of plaster whiteware into a colored object of beauty. You see, it is your handiwork that turns plaster into plaster*craft!*

Index